"Suzy Martyn's book, *Sleep Tight*, is just what the doctor ordered! As a physician and a mother, I sympathize with exhausted parents who struggle to get their little ones to nap soundly during the day and sleep uninterrupted through the night. With humor, wisdom, and compassion, Suzy offers a practical, easy-to-follow blueprint for parents to help their children get the sleep they must have to be healthy and happy. In our sleep-deprived society, it's never too early to create a solid foundation for a good night's rest."

-Rallie McAllister, M.D., MPH, MSEH

"Sleepless nights are officially over! I have to say that I was a skeptic when I first heard about the techniques in *Sleep Tight*. I had read just about every book on sleep and did not find anything that worked. After just a few days of applying Suzy's plan, I don't even recognize my daughter. She says 'goodnight and bye-bye' to us at the door and then quietly puts her head down and falls asleep! A dream? No, just a solution that works!"

-Jeff Arenzana, School Counselor and Father of 2

"Suzy was with us from the very first few days of our son's life. With her by our side, she guided us step by step into a nice routine that helped us anticipate and tend to his needs. We found ourselves calm, confident, and with more time to enjoy our son rather than spend time guessing what his needs were. At three months, he is sleeping through the night!"

-Jeannie Craft, Family Therapist and Mother of 1

"I enjoyed Suzy's approachable, welcoming style. Her writing is clear and easy to understand—perfect for a sleep-deprived mom. Suzy handles this touchy topic with kindness and sensitivity. I liked that *Sleep Tight* presents one simple goal: for parents who want to teach their child to sleep on his own and stay asleep in his own bed all night long, as well as take good, restorative naps during the day. I also appreciated that *Sleep Tight* presents a simple plan and clear, actionable advice that even an exhausted mom could follow. She also offers plenty of unique advice that I never thought of. Brilliant!"

-Jennifer Bright Reich, founder and editorial director of
MommyMDGuides.com

"There's no question that my husband's and my quality of life has improved dramatically! My husband wants to erect a Suzy Shrine in our house! We believe our son is happier, too. We didn't know what we were missing! My husband and I are simply thrilled!"

-Alicia Tulloch, Mother of 1

"Finally, we found something that worked! On the first day of the plan, our daughter actually put herself to sleep for both naps and even back to sleep after waking for the afternoon nap! She is now sleeping 12 hours at night and taking 2-hour naps after working with Suzy. Suzy has made a HUGE difference in our lives. The grass is greener on the other side of this fence!"

-Kerry Patterson, Nurse and Mother of 1

"Why did we wait this long? Our fifteen-month-old daughter was waking up in the middle of the night almost every night, needing to be rocked back to sleep. Sometimes we couldn't get her to fall back asleep even after trying to give her milk and we'd be up for hours in the middle of the night. When we followed Suzy's advice, we had a couple hard nights of training. We couldn't believe that by the third night, just like Suzy said, our daughter slept through the entire night. Our entire family began getting the sleep we needed."

-Janice Wong, Elementary School Teacher and Mother of 2

"I used the methods in Sleep Tight as a last resort. I knew I wanted to help our eighteen-month-old son to sleep, but I needed someone to walk me through step by step and encourage me along the way. Suzy's plan is so simple and it works! In just a few short days, my son has done a complete turnaround. He sleeps through the night and has lengthened his daily naps. I am expecting my second child now and will definitely put all of Suzy's advice to practice early on. I will not wait until this one is eighteen months old!"

-Kelly Geissman, Elementary School Teacher and Mother of 2

Sleep Tight

Sleep Tight

Help Your Child Attain
a Good Night's Sleep in Three Days

Suzy Martyn

Mother's Friend Publishing
Cypress, CA

Mother's Friend Publishing
P.O. Box 1020, Cypress, CA 90630.
www.MothersFriendSOS.com

Design: Hi Fidelity Graphics

Publisher's Cataloging-In-Publication Data
(Prepared by The Donohue Group, Inc.)

Martyn, Suzy.
    Sleep tight : help your child attain a good night's sleep in three days /
Suzy Martyn.

        p. : ill. ; cm.

    Includes index.
    ISBN: 978-0-578-00952-0

1. Infants~Sleep~Popular works. 2. Toddlers~Sleep~Popular works. 3. Sleep-wake cycle~Popular works. I. Title.

BF720.S53 M378 2009
154.6

Mother's Friend
Support. Equip. Inspire. Enjoy!

To all the precious little ones who are now
Sleeping Tight

And to all those who will soon join them in
Sweet Slumber

Contents

PART THREE: Smoothing out the Wrinkles
Handling Challenges

Sleep my child and peace attend thee,
All through the night
Guardian angels God will send thee,
All through the night
Soft the drowsy hours are creeping,
Hill and dale in slumber sleeping,
I my loved ones' watch am keeping,
All through the night

PART ONE:

Getting Equipped

The Foundations for Sleep Success

"Now I Lay Me Down to Sleep"

Introduction

Within minutes of waking in the morning, I can tell if my husband has gotten enough sleep the night before. Smiles and lighthearted jokes don't come as quickly, and his usual peppy step is missing. His patience for my chatter or requests for help are not as easy to come by. And that's just after having one bad night of sleep!

I remember when we had our first newborn in the house and my husband was so kind to wake with me every three hours to help with feeding, burping, and diaper changes. One night I decided to let him sleep the whole night through and take care of the nighttime routine myself. I thought perhaps even though he was not fully awakened, he would still notice the two times that I had fed, burped, and changed our daughter, but in the morning he exclaimed, to my amusement, "Wow, she slept through the night, huh?"

We all need sleep. We need deep, uninterrupted hours of sleep at night and sufficient rest during the day in order to function at our best. In order to focus on our work, manage our households, and spend quality time with friends and family, we need to start the day with a rested and refreshed body, mind, and soul.

Chances are if your child is not sleeping tight throughout the night on his own then neither are you. Both of you are in dire need of rest. You are not functioning at optimal levels during the day, and you need this book as much as your child does. If you are not able to leave your child for the night with a kiss and gentle whispering of, "Sleep tight, don't let the bedbugs bite," then you need the hope provided here on the following pages. Read on.

Welcome!

Perhaps you come to this book as a new parent who is afraid to make any mistakes and wants to get it right from the start. You've come to the right place. Or it could be that you are a parent of a ten-month-old who hasn't learned the art of sleeping. Right place again. Or, you might be a seasoned parent of multiple children and you have not had a good night's sleep in years. Perhaps you have a friend or a daughter who desperately needs to hear a voice of reason in this emotional roller coaster of teaching your children the art of sleep. Welcome all.

We all know that sleep deprivation can affect one's disposition. But parents are often surprised to find that once their child is getting the rest she needs, she is no longer as grumpy or disagreeable as before. **What was once considered a 'personality trait' is discovered to be no more than a side effect of sleep deprivation.**

Consider this story involving a Colorado mom with whom I was consulting. During our initial interview the mom was telling me that her five-month-old daughter would get very irritated and impatient with the simplest of activities. Even pulling a shirt over her head while trying to dress her would sometimes send her into frantic tears. Immediately after her daughter began getting sufficient rest during naps and at nighttime, this happy mom reported to me that her daughter no longer fussed over this simple task of dressing. In fact, the mom began to be able to predict her daughter's reaction based on the amount of sleep she got that day. She used to think her daughter was just fussy about dressing, but she realized that it was just her sleep-deprived state that brought tears easily and made it hard to be cooperative with even the simplest of tasks.

A Sleep Crisis

I hate to be the bearer of bad news, but you need to know that we 21st Century Americans are in the midst of a sleep crisis. It doesn't make the news as often as our national struggle with obesity, but it's just as real and just as serious. It's a crisis that is easy to overlook, because it's so widespread. What's normal is not what's best. One survey found that children of all age groups are on average being shortchanged an hour of sleep or more every night. It's an epidemic that is impacting infants, school-age kids, teens, and adults. We're a nation of zombie insomniacs, and it's time for us to wake up and smell the highly caffeinated beverage of our choice![1]

Sleep deprivation affects a child's disposition by making him irritable, impatient, fussy, overly sensitive, and tearful. But if this were just about cranky kids and groggy parents, it wouldn't be such a big issue. The fact is that lack of sleep has been linked to a

---

[1] One of many studies that shed light on the ill effects of sleep deprivation was conducted at Northwestern University, as reported in the article "Study: Sleep-deprived Kids Get Fat," Nancy Helmich, USA Today, 2/7/2007.

vast array of physical and psychological troubles. Here's a partial list:

(Obesity
(Hindered physical development
(Lowered physical immunities
(Learning disabilities
(Negative self-image
(Depression
(Behavioral problems
(Stress on the family

If you have a child now, take a look at the chart below and see if he or she is close to the recommended amount of sleep.[2] You will notice that the hours needed goes down very gradually. These

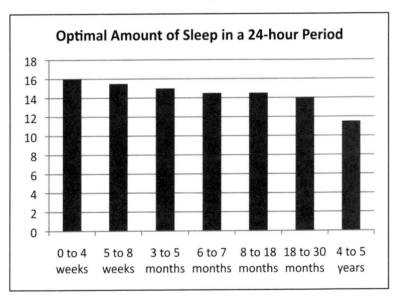

Optimal Amount of Sleep in a 24-hour Period

---

[2] In this and all sleep recommendations in this book, we allow for a reasonable degree of variation- up to an hour more or less that the indicated average per 24-hour period.

are averages, so your child could need up to an hour more or less than what is listed. However, if you have, for instance, a seven-month-old who is only sleeping a total of 8 hours a day, chances are you will notice that he seems easily agitated and generally disagreeable most of the day. Consider that this is a result of sleep deprivation rather than a personality trait.

It is part of our job as parents to ensure that our child gets enough rest. In conjunction with healthy activity, cognitive stimulation, proper nutrition, loving touch and words, vision and direction for their lives, teaching our child the art of sleep is an essential piece of the puzzle in this journey of parenting.

Sleep-Deprived Child:	Well-Rested Child:
☹ Easily irritated	☺ Playful and patient
☹ Unpredictable crying outbursts	
☹ Distractible	☺ Able to focus for extended periods of time and complete puzzles and other tasks
☹ Clumsy	
☹ Has trouble focusing on a task	
☹ Clingy	☺ Can play alone happily for lengthy periods of time
☹ Wants to be held all day	
☹ Whiny	☺ Open-minded
☹ Close-minded	☺ Cooperative
☹ Generally disagreeable	
☹ Falls asleep whenever in the car or stroller	☺ Alert and awake on outings

Has your child been labeled as a "poor sleeper?" Have you been told that she just might only need 7 hours of sleep at night?

Are you convinced that she is beyond help? Is it hard to imagine things being any different?

Once a child is getting the regular rest he needs, parents will see change on many levels: a child who is happier, more contented, and overall more agreeable. He will be more focused, attentive, and function at higher levels physically, mentally, and emotionally. What's more, parents will be better rested and happier, too! They will be enjoying quiet evenings with loved ones, reading luxurious novels during naptime, finding sanity and extra time to perhaps even dust off photo albums. You will be enjoying life more as it was intended.

That's the good news: regardless of your circumstances, and no matter what others may have told you, it is not too late. The approach introduced in this book can help produce results. Of course, everyone's circumstance is different. You may find that you can tackle this problem overnight. Or you may encounter a few wrinkles that require some perseverance and resolve. Either way, as long as you're committed to making a change, you can be confident that the end result will be a healthier and happier family.

Where did this "Sleep Solution" come from?

I have had the privilege of working on the issue of sleep with so many wonderful families over the course of my time as a parenting consultant. I'm always inspired by the way that the parents' love for their child manifests itself in their determination to go the extra mile and give them the very best care that they can give.

This book contains much of the same advice and techniques that I use with those parents. It worked for them, and it will work for you. Here you will discover a fresh, clear, and easy-to-understand look at the topic of sleep. The methods presented are simply outlined for easy understanding. There are step-by-step instructions, practical examples, and additional assistance for special circumstances based on the most frequently asked questions regarding sleep.

It's often helpful to hear about the struggles and successes of other parents. Unfortunately, we don't often get the chance to get together and share those stories with each other. So in part two of the book I've included a few **"Tales from the Trenches."** In these real-life stories, we will have the privilege of getting a peek into the lives of a diverse group of different families and their experience with teaching their child to fall asleep on his own. Although the plan and outcome was very similar for each family, everyone's actual experience was particular to their situation. Some found their babies quickly slipping right into the routine with ease, while others struggled through months before they saw complete success. In every case, however, the end result was a child who was on a predictable routine where he was falling asleep on his own and getting enough rest during the day and night to function happily and contentedly throughout the day.

(Note: The names in these case studies and circumstances not essential to outcome have been changed to protect the privacy of the families represented here.)

If at any point you feel that you need additional help and support, please head over to www.MothersFriendSOS.com. There you'll find more sleep resources, an interactive blog, and, best of all, a direct line to the author! I would love to hear about your own situation and story, so feel free to send me an email anytime.

What's Your Angle?

You've very possibly had the experience of standing in the parenting aisle of your local bookstore, bewildered by the plethora of options when it comes to sleep books. If you dig into a few of those books, you'll discover that there are many different and even contradictory approaches to the issue of sleeping babies. Each of those approaches has its merits and value. So what makes this book different, and what philosophical point of view am I coming from? Fair question. To start with, I hold these truths near and dear:

(*Sleep is something of a lost art in our culture, and it deserves to be rediscovered.*

(*Sleep training isn't rocket science, but it does help to have some basic facts under your belt.*

(*Routine: babies thrive on it.*

(*Parenting is meant to be enjoyed.*

Next, the values below have guided the way that the material in this book is presented:

(**Accessibility.** *Busy parents need to get at the material quickly. So I've cut out the filler and given you lots of charts, tables and checklists.*

(**Bias-free.** *No hidden agendas here, just solid medical research, real-life experiences, and the desire to give our kids the healthy and happy start to life that they deserve.*

(**Community.** *It takes a village, and our web community and one-on-one consulting will keep you connected and supported.*

Finally, one overarching goal: **This book is for parents who want to teach their child to sleep on his own and stay asleep in his own bed all night long, as well as take good, restorative naps during the day.** That's the simple bottom line by which we'll measure our success.

Hang In There, Baby!

You've heard the saying "it's harder on the parent than the child." That is definitely true in the case of sleep training. I've come across many reluctant parents for whom this process has taken its toll. But while the parent winces and cringes, the baby (after drying a few tears, perhaps) comes out of it smiling and happier than ever. The end result makes the hard part so worthwhile.

In my work with families, I've managed to identify the one factor that will determine the outcome of this endeavor: it's the perseverance of the parents. It could very well require some resolve, will power, and faith to see this process through.

The church down the street posted this saying on its marquee last week: "Obstacles are the fearful things you see when you take your eyes off the goal." As cliché as that is, it certainly applies to this endeavor. My husband (the sometimes-cranky guy I mentioned at the beginning of the chapter) is currently training to run his first marathon. Running 26.2 miles is something he never before would have thought possible. But he has a training routine laid out by an experienced coach. Some days he feels as if he's flying a few inches off the ground, while more often he feels like bricks are tied to his feet. Either way, he gets out there and follows the program. A clear goal, a trustworthy coach, and the determination to keep going.

Take a moment and think about what you'd like to see change in your family's daily routine. Don't be afraid to be specific, and don't be afraid to be ambitious. In fact, go ahead and write down your goal (or goals) on a note page at the back of this book. Good. Now you're one step closer to sleeping tight!

Sleep Tight

It may be difficult to imagine a different reality in your family. But you're surrounded by those who have travelled this road before, so be encouraged, have hope, and hang in there!

So let's get to work. In the next chapter we'll confront the three most common "sleep myths."

Here's to the beginning of the journey!

2

"Feeling Drowsy"

Sleep Myths and Misconceptions

Walk into any room with a group of parents, especially moms, and chances are it won't be long before someone mentions something about sleep. People seem to always have something to say or ponder (or complain) about this topic.

Although much good can come from discussions of this sort, it is important to be able to discern fact from fiction. Just because there exists a commonly held belief, that does not mean it is necessarily true. **When working to help our children attain good sleep habits, it is crucial to come to the table with accurate information.**

In this chapter we're going to shed the light of truth on the three most common sleep myths.

Myth #1: Children instinctively know when and how much sleep they need in order to be healthy and to thrive.

Somewhere along the way, parents have been told that babies will sleep when they are sleepy, eat when they are hungry, and wake when it's time to play and that they somehow magically know what is best for them. Parents are led to believe that sleep will come naturally because it is, after all, a natural thing. It is true that for some babies everything does seem to come easily and naturally, but for many children, guidance and direction is needed from someone who has their best interests at heart.

What would happen if each night before bedtime I drove you around the block until you fell asleep, and if every time you stirred in the middle of the night, I handed you a glass of warm milk or the remote to the television to lull you back to sleep? How many nights do you think it would take for you to develop the habit to wake and expect those very things at the same times each night? Would you awake each morning rested and alert and full of energy for the day?

Although you might have achieved a total of eight hours of sleep each night, because of the frequent lengthy wakings, you would not have been able to get into the deep REM (rapid eye movement) sleep that is necessary for full healthy sleep. The assistance that you received to fall asleep might have appeared to be helpful initially, but in the end, it really was a disservice to you.

Just as in the above example with adults, we need to teach our children to sleep at night and stay asleep all night. We also need to teach them to get the rest they need during the day, especially when they are infants. **When their natural wakings mid-nap or in the middle of the night become invitations to get up and eat** or to play, we need to graciously decline. When their cries com-municate that they know what they want, we need to gently remind them that we know what is best for them in the long run. Rather than trusting our child's instincts, we need to plan and guide our children into healthy patterns. And doing so is one of the most loving things we can do for them.

Myth #2: Sleep schedules and sleep training harm children developmentally and emotionally.

Parents are often told that only what comes "naturally" is good for a child, so they often conclude that intentionally teaching children specific sleep habits interferes with a child's natural ten-dencies. They're afraid that schedules are too restrictive and somehow detrimental for the child.

For example, if their child is only taking thirty-minute naps, then the parents may be tempted to conclude that it must be be-cause that's all she needs in order to be refreshed and restored. They don't understand that while it's true that their child is stirring at that time because it is a natural waking interval, that doesn't nec-essarily mean that it should be the end of the naptime. When parents see that the child is needing to be held for some time after her short nap and isn't ready to play happily, that should be an in-dicator of a truncated nap. But they don't always make that connection, because they're too willing to accept what's 'natural.'

Although it is true that there are many natural tendencies in children that are to be embraced, a child's ability to monitor, evaluate, and train himself towards a healthy sleep routine is not always realistic or wise. Of course, there are children that naturally fall into good routines (some parents get all the luck!), but the rest of us cannot depend on chance for this to occur. We must feel confident in the knowledge that our children need our guidance and that teaching them is part of being a loving parent.

Myth #3: No one method or routine works for all children. Most children will not conform to sleep averages and standards.

Children come in all shapes and sizes and with different personalities and preferences. Parents can honor a child's individuality by providing different enrichment activities, opportunities, discipline and experiences, but the fact remains that every child's basic need for regular restorative sleep should not be overlooked or denied. A predictable sleep routine is not something one child needs and another can do without. **Sleep is a basic need in life for everyone.**

In the plans that follow, we will allow for a reasonable amount of flexibility, both from child to child and from one day to the next. But let's agree that it is a rare exception to find a child who completely thrives to his utmost potential without getting sufficient sleep day after day and night after night.

Having lain to rest some oft-heard fiction, it's time to get to the facts. In the next chapter we'll get a crash course on everything you need to know about the inner workings of sleep.

3

"Drifting Off"

It's as Easy as R-E-M

If you are reading this book, I can assume that your child needs more sleep. He is either not sleeping through the night or unable to settle to take substantial, restorative daytime naps in which he wakes happy and refreshed. You have experienced the negative effects of sleep deprivation on your child and the family, and you are ready to see change. You've realized that sleep does not come naturally to all. You want your child to sleep tight. You are literally tired of the effects of sleep deprivation not only on your child but your entire family.

You might come with all sorts of worries including wondering if you are doing the right thing, if your child is ready, if it's going to work, or whether you have the will to really give it a try. It's normal to have doubts. However, if you wait until you are absolutely sure and have no hint of doubt at all, chances are it will be a long wait. And, in the meantime, you and your child are continuing to lose more nights of sleep as you wait and wonder. Let's put it this way: **I have yet to come across a single parent who is sorry that their previously sleepless child is now sleeping soundly on their own all night long.** In other words, it might be a tough road, but it will be worth it in the end.

With commitment, consistency, and support, you can make the change that you've been longing for.

Proceed With Caution

It's necessary to take a few things to heart before we begin. As you enter into this process with an open mind, always take seriously your instincts and intuitions as a parent. You have been selected to the best parent for your child and you know him better than anyone else. If at any point you don't feel right about something or if you feel a need to check in with a doctor, please address the situation without hesitation. You can always come back to your plan later, but it is important to have all the facts before continuing.

Having said that, if you are committed to giving something a try, then give it a fair shot. Be consistent and follow-through decisively. That is the only way to know for sure whether something is going to work or not. Also, surround yourself with people who will support you, have experience and knowledge, and who believe in what you are doing.

In all you do, think "big picture." The approach shared in this book can be applied to many aspects of parenting aside from purely teaching sleep skills. Don't get discouraged by the difficulty of the short-term and lose sight of where you want to be long-term.

Lastly, embrace the entire process as you enter in with resolve and commitment. Learn from the mistakes around each corner and celebrate each and every one of the small successes along the way.

Sleep 101

In Chapter 1 we discussed the vital importance of getting enough sleep. Closely tied to the issue of sleep *quantity* is the idea of the *quality*, or I should say *qualities* of sleep.

There are two major types of sleep: REM and NREM. The first type, REM (rapid eye movement) is when you do most of your active dreaming and is characterized by the active movement of your eyes going back and forth (hence the name). NREM (non-REM) sleep consists of four stages through which a person travels into progressively deeper sleep. Achieving sleep at each of the different stages is vital to a person's health and overall well-being. It is very normal to wake briefly or enter into lighter stages of sleep while transitioning from one type of sleep to another. If there is no stimulation at these transitional times, deeper sleep naturally follows.[3]

Let's take a look at each of these stages.

Drowsiness

In this first stage you can be very easily awakened. It is the shortest stage, lasting only up to 10 minutes. A drowsy child's eyes move slowly under the eyelids. His muscle activity begins to slow down.

---

[3] The classic research on sleep cycles and stages was done by Rechtschaffen and Kales in 1968. More recently scientists have actually observed REM sleep in a fetus. Which leads one to wonder: what could a child who has yet to be born possible be dreaming about?

Light Sleep

During light sleep, there is a halt of eye movement. The heart rate slows at this point and the body temperature slowly decreases. Breathing becomes deeper and more regular and there might be sudden muscle contractions. This is when some children experience sleepwalking, fitful tossing and turning, night terrors, or bed-wetting.

Deep Sleep

There are two stages of deep sleep and one is very difficult to wake during these stages. If awoken at this stage, a child would feel very groggy, disoriented, and it would take some time to become mentally alert. This stage is a crucial time where one's brain requires less blood flow, thereby allowing muscles an extra burst of blood flow. This helps to restore physical energy and it has even been shown that immune functions increase during deep sleep.

REM Sleep

After about an hour or hour and a half of being asleep, infants enter into REM sleep. About 50% of sleep is REM sleep for infants. Breathing is rapid, irregular, and shallow. This stage is associated with relieving stress, retaining memory, and processing emotions. It is even said that during this time the brain is developing the ability to learn and develop new skills. This REM sleep stage is the most crucial of all the stages and it is the stage that a body will crave and attempt to recover if it is sleep deprived.

The chart that follows maps out a typical night of sleep for an average adult. Young children will move through those cycles more quickly, but the idea remains that our minds and bodies were designed to use a full night of uninterrupted sleep to get recharged.

For children who are receiving multiple interventions at night or during naps, it is very difficult to get the healthy, restora-

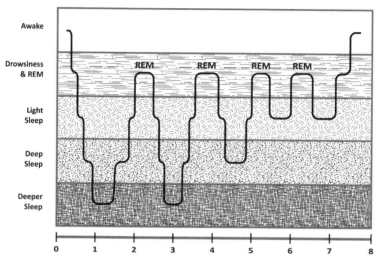

tive sleep that comes at the deep sleep and REM stages. Instead, children are going in and out of light sleep and therefore are not waking restored and refreshed as you might hope. They are not receiving the full benefits of sleep.

Average Daytime and Nighttime Sleep

If you're a visual learner type, you might appreciate the chart on the following page. The darker line represents hours of sleep during the night, while the lighter gray bars are daytime naps. Notice how a child progresses from nearly equal amounts of day and night sleep to the point where he will drop his afternoon nap and sleep only at night. As mentioned earlier, the total amount of sleep during a 24-hour period changes very gradually.

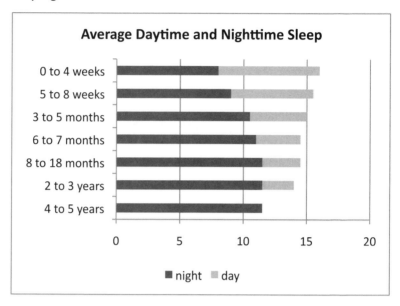

Average Daytime and Nighttime Sleep

Since REM sleep is the gold standard of sleep, if you will, it's only fitting that our three steps to success follow the acronym "R-E-M." For our purposes, those letters will stand for **Routine, Expectations, and Mood.** Taken together, those three steps form our basic strategy to help your child sleep tight. If you establish a routine, set realistic but firm expectations, and set a mood that is conducive to sleep, then you'll be well on your way to sleep success. Let's take a closer look at each element.

Routine-
In a groove, but not a rut

Routines are crucial in a child's life. A child can benefit from having regularity and predictability to his days and nights regardless of personality or temperament. Within the structure of such routine, there is ample room for flexibility and spontaneity, but coming back to routines is very comforting for a child. It increases his sense of stability and security and creates the framework for his days and nights.

Daytime Routine

Many parents find that once they establish a good daytime rhythm of rest and play that the nighttime sleep comes much more naturally. A child who is over-stimulated during the day does not rest as well at night. Contrary to popular belief, a child will not sleep better at night because he has gotten little sleep during the day. The overtiredness or over-stimulation from a day actually hinders a child's ability to enter into nighttime sleep in a calm and relaxed manner. **Good sleep leads to better sleep. An overtired child does not make up for lost sleep during the day by sleeping more soundly and longer at night. In fact, he is less likely to fall asleep easily or stay asleep for long periods of time.**

Be sure to limit over-stimulation during the day, especially if the prior day has been very active. Most babies do well with a good dose of daily down time. As a general guideline, babies under 3 months of age probably would do best with a maximum of one outing or visit a day. In the next few months, you could gradually add more, but at all times, tune into your baby and takes cues from extra fussiness, inability to settle for naps, or seeming too active or interactive. These are all signs that it's time to slow down. Of course, take into account your baby's personality and tolerance for change.

For older children, it is also important to have a good balance of rest and play during the day. As you get to know your child, try a variety of activities to see what your child enjoys. Go to the gardens, take Mommy and Me classes, and schedule play dates. Sit out on the porch and watch the neighbors walk by or go on stroller walks. What could be soothing and comforting to one child could possibly be an alarming situation for another. Or, you may discover your child has a passion for being outdoors. The only way you will know these things is if you make it a regular routine to expose your child to different activities, environments, and people. It's good for child and parent.

Nap Routine

As you balance your days with enjoyable activities, it's important to give your child the rest he needs as well. It may feel like your child does not need naps because he seems so involved in what he is doing, but every child needs a good balance of rest and play. If he is going from one activity to another, it's possible that what is interpreted as a "second wind" is actually over-stimulation, which can hinder a child's ability to enter into a calm and drowsy state. What can result is an over-tired child who will sleep fitfully. He needs the rest, but is so worked up from the activities of the day that it is difficult to relax even with a bedtime routine.

Naptime routines should be brief, lasting for no more than 20 minutes. Some children require only a few minutes before being ready to settle down for a nap. Snuggling on the couch with one calming story is all that is needed in many cases. If you extend this time too long, your efforts can actually backfire. Your child can become over-stimulated and get a second wind, thereby appearing to have lost the need for sleep.

Nighttime Routine

Be sure to establish a nice bedtime routine that your child can anticipate and look forward to. Consider a bath, soothing song, and/or a massage. Often times, it's helpful to agree ahead of time on the number of books that you will read or even select the books ahead of time to streamline the process. It can become wearisome for some parents to read the exact same books in the exact same order every single night for an entire year, but your child finds great comfort and security in this routine. Allow him that luxury.

When my youngest daughter was just thirteen months old, she would bring out the same three books each night to read. She knew what order we read them, as well. If I tried to mix it up a bit and change the words or read out of order, she would look at me with a confused look on her face. I learned quickly that this evening routine was very soothing and special for her. Although reading the same books in the same order each night wasn't my first choice, it was what helped soothe her into being ready to drift off for the night. And, who wants to get in the way of that?

Sample Bedtime Routine
For a Two-Year-Old

7:00 p.m.	Bath (Sometimes extended bath times can hinder the flow of the bedtime routine, so during this time of training, limit bath times to 20 minutes.)
7:20 p.m.	Change into pajamas, Brush teeth
7:30 p.m.	Read three short stories (Consider books that end with the character going to bed.)
7:40 p.m.	Bedtime prayers and final hugs. Often times children will attempt to extend this time as much as possible. Be brief and talk positively about the new day ahead.
7:45 p.m.	Off to dreamland...

Keep your bedtime routine to 30 or 45 minutes. Any longer and it can drag on indefinitely, any shorter and it doesn't allow time to get adjusted to the idea of sleep. You will find that once your child gets accustomed to the idea of a bedtime routine, she will actually welcome and look forward to it as she anticipates the comfort of dreamland.

Remember that the sample routine on the previous page is just that: a sample. Your routine will likely differ from this, and that's fine. You may find that it works better to do baths in the morning, or that an older toddler has the attention span for 15 or 20 minutes of reading. Know that with this and all other schedules presented here, you have the final say as to what is working and what needs to change.

From "Expecting" to "Expectations"

All three of my daughters are quite friendly, but one is shyer than the others. It takes more effort for her to reach out to strangers, especially when attempting to initiate conversation. Even while taking this fact into consideration, our **expectation** as parents is the same for all three girls: When you see someone, you greet them. Whether with a smile, wave, or by offering of your entire life story, you acknowledge people's presence with friendliness. It's tempting to excuse one girl from expressing herself this way because of her personality. It may feel unkind to require her to do something that is so difficult for her. However, it's more about common courtesy than what comes naturally or easily. All members of the family together strive to be polite and courteous to all they encounter. One does not get excused because being polite is uncomfortable. It's a **standard** we all uphold despite our personality differences.

Standards are important because they help us to stick to things that we know are right and healthy. What would happen if we could drive at any age, park anywhere we pleased, and abolished all speed limits or driving laws? What if we said, "Oh, it's inhibiting John's freedom to express himself if we require him to drive on just one side of the street." I don't think any of us would enjoy living in that sort of chaos, that is if we survived long enough to make that judgment. The world functions and thrives with order, and our personal lives need a healthy dose of this as well. Our children need this very early in their lives and it's a parent's job to provide an orderly environment.

It is true that every baby is an individual and will have different needs, personalities, and styles. Some babies enjoy more stimulation while others thrive in a quieter environment. One baby might love to be held by strangers while another wants to stay close to mom. But again, the expectations that we are setting for our child are standards that transcend individual personality, and will ultimately allow him to blossom into the fullness of the person that he was created to be.

One day I instructed a two-year-old to put away a toy. He looked up at me and with his big blue eyes said "But, I can't *want* to do it." My reply was, "Oh! You don't have to *want* to do it, you just *have* to do it!" With confusion in his eyes as to how this could be the case, but with the understanding of the bottom line (i.e., I must comply), he slowly but surely walked up to the toy and put it away.

What would you do if your child simply could not stand taking baths nor brushing her teeth? Would you allow her to go days and even weeks without taking care of these very important tasks? What if she refused to eat any vegetables or fruit and insisted on having pasta for every meal seven days a week? Would you go ahead and plan macaroni and cheese for the whole month?

As a responsible parent who knows what is necessary for basic hygiene and health, you require your child to adhere to basic standards for his own benefit. Even if he cried during every tooth brushing, you would still require him to do it because the simple fact is he needs those teeth for the rest of his life. Whether or not he likes to eat anything nutritious, he needs to do so, and therefore you hold him to that standard.

In the same way that we have safety, health and hygiene guidelines, in the interest of our child's overall well-being, we can and should set a standard for our children in the arena of sleep. There is a healthy average of sleep that every child needs, and it is our job as parents to insure that he gets what he needs. Children thrive with a predictable routine and schedule. **Knowing what to expect is comforting for both child and parent and takes much of the guesswork out of parenting.**

Suzy's Tip #1:

White Noise

Many parents express concern over their baby's cries waking an older sibling. To help with this situation, it's a good idea to use a fan, humidifier, radio, or wave machine to block out extraneous noises throughout nap and nighttime. It works really well to bring along such devices on trips while in unfamiliar places so that your child has some consistency, comfort, and level of familiarity.

Setting the Mood

Creating the right environment for restful slumber is an important part of the package. Just as you wouldn't want to send your child out to play outside without comfortable weather and clothing, so you need to prepare your child and his surroundings for the best possible experience with sleep. Here is a list of things to consider:

☾ Check the temperature in your child's room. Is it comfortable for you? What feels right to you is right for your child.

☾ Think about how your child is dressed. Is she sweating in three layers of clothing while you are sleeping in just a light t-shirt?

☾ Evaluate whether there is too much or too little light, or if the bed is positioned in a place where the first morning light is shining on your child's face.

☾ Consider noises. Do you need a fan, humidifier, radio, or other white noise to block out disturbances from outdoors or other rooms?

☾ Think about your child's environment during the bedtime routine. It should be dim and quiet with limited quick and stimulating movements. Remember that you are gradually preparing for him to get to a drowsy state.

☾ Do you have a video monitor set somewhere where you can see her entire crib or bed? Having access to a quick view of your child can be very useful. Just make sure to keep the volume down so as not to exaggerate insignificant sounds.

Simple, but not Easy

Having made the case for clear expectations and a predictable routine, I don't want you to get the idea that life has to be boring and humdrum at every turn! There is plenty of room for fun and surprises, flexibility and adjustment along the way. However, only in the context of an overall sense of calm and peace can the spontaneity of unexpected events be fully enjoyed.

Yes, I am offering a simple solution to teaching your child to sleep, but no one said that "simple" is the same as "easy." For the blessed few, it may seem to happen magically, but we are not talking about magic formulas, quick fixes, or a paint-by-numbers method that parents should follow blindly. Everything good in parenting comes with a mix of advice, insight, testing, more input, and then trial and error. Take time to really understand each situation and plan wisely, purposefully, and with openness and flexibility.

Suzy's Tip #2:

Soothing Baby Bath Routine

Many babies find a soothing bath to be the perfect transition from a long day to a long, peaceful night of rest. If, however, your baby does not find baths enjoyable and relaxing, then plan to bathe him/her outside the bedtime routine.

Suggested Order of Cleaning at Bath Time

The basic rule of thumb is to bathe the cleanest part of the body first and gradually end with the area that needs the most cleaning.

1. Wash baby's face

2. Wash baby's hair and ears (Don't forget the back of the ears!)

3. Wash legs and arms

4. Wash stomach and back

5. Take care of circumcised area

6. Wash diaper area

4

"Don't Let the Bedbugs Bite"

The Language of Tears

We're almost ready to put our plan into action. But before the sheep start soaring over your baby's crib, we'll review the most important points that we've covered so far, and address one of the more challenging but inevitable realities of sleep training: crying.

As long as you didn't doze off during the first three chapters, then you already know the most important facts about sleep, as well as the strategies that we'll use to get to the "promised land." Just in case, let's lay out a quick recap:

☾ Everyone needs sleep, especially the deep REM sleep that happens an hour or so into the sleep cycle.

☾ Establishing a predictable **routine** of feeding – waketime – sleep will bring order to your days and nights, but allow for flexibility too.

☾ Setting and enforcing reasonable **expectations** is good common-sense parenting, and won't damage your child's psyche in any way.

☾ Creating a **mood** that's conducive to sleep will make send your child the right signals, and make the routine feel natural.

☾ The key to success is your resolve and perseverance.

You may be asking: "How long is this going to take?" Fair question. The good news is that you could be experiencing long uninterrupted nights of sleep within a day or two, most likely by day 3, especially if your baby is under 6 months of age. The older your child, the longer it can take. For children as old as 10-12 months, it could take a couple weeks. And then there are other factors that can either delay or make this change more challenging, but we will cover all of that in Part Three. Regardless of how long it takes, success is entirely possible. Have hope.

If you have the luxury of a week, then that is ideal. But all you really need is a good solid weekend. Start Friday and by Monday morning you will wake with a smile on your face. Plan to stay close to home and avoid outings in stroller or car within 30 minutes of nap or nighttime. Avoid catnaps as much as possible.

Bedtime Routine

We spoke earlier about what we do just before bedtime. But it's such a crucial (and precious) moment that it's worth a more detailed run-through.

About 30 to 45 minutes before bed, begin by establishing a soothing evening routine. If baths are relaxing for your baby, start with that. Then move to a reading time or enjoy a quiet music time where you can sit together, rock and cuddle. Tempting as it might be, be careful not to let your baby doze deep into dreamland at this point. Likewise, avoid over-stimulation at this point. No tickle fests or stimulating videos. Also, to keep things simple and predictable, read the same couple of books, sing the same songs, and say the same things before final tuck-in. These things will bring predictability and routine to your child's evening and he will find it comforting. As time progresses, you will probably begin to notice your child anticipating each part of your routine. He will find comfort in this, and it will prepare him for a good night's rest.

Your child should be calm and drowsy, but not asleep at this point. Be quick, matter-of-fact, and with reassuring words, put your child down quickly and walk out of the room without hesitation. If you are reluctant, stressed, or worried, your child will pick up on this. Act naturally and your child will pick up on your confidence and the expectation that this is a normal and regular part of your daily routine.

This is the most important part. Check the monitor, and then go do something that takes 15 to 20 minutes like laundry, bills, or a phone call. If at some point you hear a cry of distress, check the monitor again. If you need to assist in some way, then do so, but do it quickly and limit interaction.

If all is well when you check the monitor, then go do something else that takes about 15 to 20 minutes.

The good news is that for most people, it doesn't get beyond this. Their child has fallen asleep. Don't be discouraged by the fact that perhaps your child has been perspiring or that it seemed emotionally difficult. It could possibly last another day or two, but the end is near.

Suzy's Tip #3:

Video Monitors

I don't know how I could have gotten along all these years without my trusty video monitor. It has served to be my eyes and ears during naps and nighttime sleep for years. Although I do not rely on it as my only source of feedback on how my child is doing, it is an invaluable tool especially during training periods and seasons of sickness. While frequently visiting and monitoring my child from the other room, the monitor helped to provide constant feedback for moments when I was not physically with my child in the same room.

Video monitors are still more expensive than their audio-only cousins, but I would encourage you to make this an accessory where you don't compromise. You'll find that you need to visualize information even more than the sound (see below). So put one on your baby registry, or borrow one from a friend, or get a refurbished one. Whatever it takes!

Volume Tip:

Unless your baby's room is on the other side of the house and you cannot hear their cry at all, turn the volume entirely down on the video monitor. Sound is amplified by the monitors and makes the situation sound more intense and loud than it usually is. Instead of constantly listening for each and every peep, try using the "15-Minute Rule." (See Suzy's Tip #4 on pg. 38)

Don't be alarmed if there seems to be some irregularity in the pattern of learning or if there is some backsliding. This is an expected part of the process and is perfectly normal.

For those who are enduring more crying than anticipated, here's an in-depth answer to a frequently asked question.

A Look at Crying

Q: "The crying really gets to me and I just don't know how to interpret what my child's needs are. Can you help?"

A: It's important for parents to be able to distinguish the different reasons for crying.

What does it mean when a child cries? Let's look at the different options. Understanding the reasons behind crying can help parents feel more confident about responding to needs.

1. Discomfort: Whether it's a wet diaper or a new tooth coming in, a cry of discomfort is something that needs attention. Assess the situation and as much as possible, try to avoid these situations by starting with a clean diaper and soothing teething pain before putting your child down for the night.

2. Distress: If your child is in physical or emotional distress, it is necessary to respond immediately. A parent can instinctively assess a cry of distress, but be careful not to project your own feelings of uneasiness about training onto a child who is merely trying to settle himself into a sleep.

3. Over-stimulation: If your child has not had sufficient rest during the day or had an over-active day, it could be he needs to relieve some of the stress by crying. Do your best to balance your child's play and rest routine during the day so that he will come to the evening with calm and readiness to go down for the night.

4. Complaint: A child who is reluctantly being taught to fall asleep on her own is usually not going to welcome this process with open arms. It's normal for a child to at least try to sway your decision by some initial challenge especially if she is used to you responding to their request. With reassuring words of your love, press on and remember that you are giving your child what she needs, not what she wants. Keep your eyes on the long-term goal. Also, keep in mind that the older your child, there is the potential that there will be more resistance. Falling asleep while sitting, standing in protest, and tears are normal parts of the process. It may seem traumatic in the short-term, but rest assured that this phase will be a distant memory very soon.

5. Settling: You can distinguish this type of crying because it's more like you are hearing 'sounds' than crying per se. It may sound like moaning, groaning, sighing, talking, and lots of moving around. Initially, you will hear much of this, but over time it should diminish to almost nothing. Some children, however, ritualistically toss around quite a bit before finding the perfect position to be comfortable in and that is just fine. (If you think your child might be excessively unsettled all night long, consult your doctor for evaluation.)

During the training period, you can feel comforted by the fact that most of the crying you will hear will be #4 and #5. Keep your own emotions in check to be sure you are evaluating your child accurately. And think about this: If your child cried in protest because he didn't want to brush his teeth would you toss out all the toothbrushes in the house and throw in the towel? Of course you wouldn't, it's a safety and health issue. Learning how to self-soothe to sleep another important lesson for your child's overall health both now and in the long run. You want to do what is best for him even if it means there will be some tears.

Suzy's Tip #4:

The 15-Minute Rule

After baby wakes mid-nap or when baby is first put down for a nap, turn up the volume and check visually on the monitor to see baby is safe and that there is nothing that would signal an emergency. Then, go do something for 15 minutes: load of laundry, sinkful of dishes, phone call, or shower. Go back to monitor and turn volume up and check visually for needs again. (Note: sometimes this second period sounds more alarming than the first...often times, it is right after this period that babies settle and drift off)

Note: Even after babies learn to sleep through the night and haven't cried for some time, they can be awakened mid-nap or in the middle of the night once again. Use this 15-minute rule again in those situations. If after a few days, the situation is not improved, look for other reasons for the change in behavior.

Another Note: Some babies do well when parents go in to reassure (quiet, no eye-contact, pat on bottom for few minutes) after the first 15 minutes, but many get more upset at this and the process needs to start over again. In this case, the best thing to do is to resist the temptation to intervene.

Two-year-old Justine was not sick. She had been a very consistent and reliable sleeper, and I had not had any problems with putting her down to sleep since I had taught her to fall asleep on her own as a four-month-old. For the first couple days after deciding to let her sleep again without assistance, I heard light crying and a faint voice calling out, "I'm crying, I'm crying" amidst the light tears. She wanted to emphasize the message that she was trying to get across with the crying. She was very aware of what she was doing. After realizing I would not give in, within a few minutes, the room was quiet and Justine was fast asleep. She woke cheerily two hours later, and the following day there were no tears at tuck-in at all.

I hope that you feel better equipped to tackle this sleep issue with good information and a calm, confident attitude. In the next section, we'll look at the sleep routines that we want to establish for each stage of your child's development. Off we go!

PART TWO:

Working the Program

Sure-Fire Sleep Routines for Each
Age and Stage

*"A good laugh and a long sleep
are the best cures in the doctor's book."*

-Irish Proverb

5

"Sleeping Like a Baby"

Birth to Two Months

Since we have established that routines are desirable for a child's healthy development, we will now look at recommended routines for each age group. These schedules have proven themselves again and again with families just like yours. Nevertheless, remember that these are general guidelines and should be understood as such. Trust your parental instinct when you feel a routine needs to be adjusted or when your child seems to fall into a different routine than expected according to his age.

Feel free to skip between sections depending on your child's age. Each chapter is not dependent on previous ones. This means that if your child is two years old and has never been on any type of schedule, it is fine to just skip to chapter 8 and get to work. Thankfully, you don't need to put them on the infant schedule and work your way up to their current age!

Birth to Four Weeks:
Rockin' Round the Clock

Most babies are born with no sense of day or night. They want to sleep all day and be awake all night. Or much to the dismay of their parents, they will treat the entire 24 hours like one long day and take short catnaps here and there. They had the freedom to do that while in the womb, so why would they think the outside world functioned any differently?

One of the jobs of a parent is to gradually introduce their baby to the natural order of healthy living. It is the parents' responsibility to guide their child to sleep at night and play during the day. Children need to know that it's healthy to have consistent rhythms of rest and play during the day and then sleep for a considerably longer chunk during the night. Many will not come to this realization on their own. They need their parents to not only model this behavior, but to create boundaries to help ensure that it happens. When babies learn to live within these guidelines, they are generally less fussy and overall more content. Also, to the surprise and pleasure of the parents, their baby's needs are more predictable. This takes much of the guesswork out of parenting in the early months, which can be a welcome relief.

If you have a newborn, congratulations on keeping your eyes open long enough to get to this section! Or perhaps you just opened up right to this page because you know that in 14 minutes your little one will be awake and demanding your attention, and you only have time to read one chapter. However you come to this chapter, read on with hope. Rest is just around the corner.

For these first two months, we will concentrate on developing a rhythm of eating, being awake, and then sleeping about every 2.5 to 3 hours from the beginning of one feeding to the beginning of the next. In other words, we start with a feeding, then get involved in activities, and finally settle down for a nap. If you can gently work into this routine, you will find your baby more contented and able to be comfortable with this stretch between feedings.

That seems straightforward enough on paper. But it's not uncommon for babies to get caught in a catch-22 type of cycle of catnaps and snacks. When babies get into a rhythm where they fall asleep at the bottle or breast, they can tend to sleep for a very short period of time. After a short thirty-minute nap, they wake up wanting to either suckle back to sleep or fill their tummies up just a bit more. Babies can get used to a "food coma" where they fall asleep because their little tummies are full and awaken when they feel empty again. What ensues is a cycle of snacking and short catnaps, which can leave baby never fully satisfied and never fully rested.

If your newborn is already headed down that road, it may seem impossible that your child could last this long, but your baby's body will adjust very quickly. It's okay to take a few days to work on stretching your baby's feedings out if she is used to more frequent feedings. It will not take long. Be patient.

The goal is to ensure your baby gets a very full and satisfying meal each time he eats. For bottle-fed babies in these first two months, aim for 3 to 4 oz. For breastfed babies, offer both breasts at each meal and aim for at least 15 to 20 minutes of total feeding time. Remember that these are averages and you should cue into your baby's signals of satisfaction and their growth. You will learn to identify when he is just snacking and when he has had enough to sustain him until the next feeding.

If it looks like baby is trying to stretch his nap into a full-blown nighttime sleep, it's okay to wake him when it's time to

begin the next cycle. Likewise, if he's drifting off mid-feeding, it's okay to keep him awake so that he can get a full meal. In time, he will naturally wake very close to the next feeding time. Many parents say that once their babies grow accustomed to this routine, they are like a clock and wake within a few minutes of feeding time regularly on their own.

If your baby feeds and then has a good period of wakefulness and then takes a nap, instead of this cycle of snacking and catnapping, she will be content longer periods of time between feedings and mom will also have a chance to get her much needed rest. Then, mom can be at her best for when her baby needs her again. This makes for a more regular and predicable routine and in time it will take much of the guesswork out of interpreting when baby is hungry and when she is tired and ready for sleep.

You can always get back on track if you need to stray from the routine for a bit. Being flexible on occasion will not sabotage the entire process as long as you are working towards a goal in the bigger picture. So, don't fret over these unexpected occurrences. They are normal and you will be able to get back on track.

Keep in mind that your baby is learning the ropes in this strange and new world. Give plenty of grace and wiggle room in this learning process. Some babies are not ready for regulation at this level until after the first few months. Have an open mind and plan to try again when they are more ready.

Your schedule might look something like the one below. This routine is based on a three-hour interval from the beginning of one feeding to the next. Breastfed newborns will likely spend some time on a 2½-hour schedule before stretching out to three hours. In that case, you would adjust the times to reflect a 2½-hour cycle, and add another feeding to each 24-hour period.

Again, you can flex it 30 minutes to one hour either way, but sticking to regular and consistent intervals is what's important. It's also fine if at this early stage, some days are off or it's not perfect clockwork. Soon you will see a pattern reliably developing.

Sample Schedule for Babies Birth to Four Weeks:

7 a.m.	Wake, eat, and play
8:00 a.m.	**Nap**
10 a.m.	Eat, play
11:00 a.m.	**Nap**
1 p.m.	Eat, play
2:00 p.m.	**Nap**
4 p.m.	Eat, play
5:00 p.m.	**Nap**
7 p.m.	Eat, bedtime routine
8:30 p.m.	**Down for the night**
12 a.m.	Midnight feeding*
3 a.m.	Second night feeding*

*For the midnight and 3 a.m. feedings, use low lights, no eye contact, feed quickly, and if your baby will tolerate it and is not bothered by diaper rashes, change only when diaper is saturated or soiled. Also, don't feel obligated to wake your baby if they sleep through this feeding earlier. As long as she is thriving and growing, it's okay for her to go 5 to 6 hours without eating at night.

Taking Notes

It's a great idea to keep a record of your baby's activity. It will help you recognize trends, identify problems, and celebrate progress and growth. We've provided a reproducible chart for such purposes in the resources section at the end of this book.

Suzy's Tip #5:

_____

Nursing Marathon

For breastfeeding moms: In those early weeks of breastfeeding, sometimes you will find by the time you finish feeding, it will be naptime again! It's not unusual for feedings to take 45min-60min. As your baby grows, the time it takes to feed will diminish and your baby will be able to have periods of wakefulness that last 15 minutes or longer. In the first few weeks of life, be careful not to have your baby up for too long (over 30 minutes) at a time as this may over-stimulate your baby and hinder her ability to settle into a nap before her next feeding.

In the end, while having this rhythm in your mind, pay attention to your baby's cues and needs for flexibility in the case of growth spurts, illnesses, or just needing more time to adjust. If she is hungry, feed her even if it is sooner than you were hoping. Afterwards, you can always get back on track for the rest of the day.

Five to Eight Weeks: Sleeping Through the Night!

In this early stage, it sometimes feels that as soon as you get used to a schedule, your baby is ready to "graduate" into the next one. You'll experience the first such transition as early as week 2 or

3, and most likely by week 5 or 6. That's when you may notice your baby is ready to drop the midnight feeding. In the next few weeks, she will quite possibly drop the 3 a.m. feeding until she is sleeping 10 to 12 hours straight at night. You might begin to notice that if she is still waking at midnight or 3 a.m. that it is more out of habit than hunger. In that case, give her ample time to fall back to sleep on her own and she should not wake at those regular times any longer after about 3 to 5 nights of not being stimulated or fed.

A landmark weight seems to be around 13 pounds, at which time babies can sleep 10 to 12 hours without food. During regular growth spurts (approx at 3 wks, 6 wks, 9 wks, 12 wks, 6 mo, 9 mo) your baby might wake at night again after having slept through the night, but it should only last 3 to 5 nights. Any longer and he might wake only out of habit or due to other causes such as illness or teething.

If your child wakes earlier than expected, do your best to hold off on feeding until close to the scheduled time, and work for the rest of the day to get back on schedule. If you find the need for flexibility one day and have to adjust the entire schedule for that day, don't worry. Just start again the following morning. If you find that you are constantly fighting early wakings, it's possible that you need to adjust your schedule or you might need to check that your child is thriving and getting enough to eat.

Sample Schedule for Babies 5 to 8 Weeks:

7:00 a.m.	Wake, eat, and play
8:30 a.m.	**Nap**
10:00 a.m.	Eat, play
11:30 a.m.	**Nap**
1:00 p.m.	Eat, play
2:30 p.m.	**Nap**
4:00 p.m.	Eat, play
5:30 p.m.	**Nap**
7:00 p.m.	Eat, bedtime routine
8:30 p.m.	**Down for the night**
12:00 a.m.	Midnight feeding*
3:00 a.m.	Second night feeding*

*As in the first month, make the late night feeding brief and mellow. By eight weeks, both of these feedings will likely be dropped.

Congratulations, you've made it through the first (and possibly most challenging) two months of your baby's life! Here's what we've been working on so far:

(*Full feedings instead of snacks.*
(*Full sleep sessions instead of catnaps.*
(*Phasing out the two late night feedings.*

If you're doing well with those three goals, then you've set up some great basic habits, and it will be relatively easy for you adjust and adapt as your child grows. If you're not on track yet, don't give up! You know by now that all children are fully capable of finding that routine, even if it takes a little longer for some than for others.

Either way, this would be a good time to flip over to Part Three. That's where we've collected some of the most common questions from parents like you.

Suzy's Tip #6:

"Growth Spurts"

After a period of sleeping so soundly on her own, my six-month-old daughter started to wake suddenly in the middle of the night. She didn't have a temperature nor did I see any signs of teething. As I agonized over this period of three nights of waking, I noticed that she was outgrowing her sleepers. Ah, ha! I remembered someone once telling me that 'growing pains' at night actually physically hurt a baby sometimes-that it was physically uncomfortable to sleep. Alas, my first experience with a growth spurt.

During a growth spurt, your baby may wake more often for feedings or feed longer than usual for a period of time. It should not last more than 3-5 days. Typical times for growth spurts are at 3 weeks, 6 weeks, 9 weeks, 12 weeks, 6 months, and 9 months although growth spurts can really happen at any time. If your child's symptoms last longer or you sense there is more to her discomfort, then consider illness or teething. Another consideration is that you and your child may need to go back and "re-work the plan."

Tales from the Trenches:

"None of These Methods Work for MY Child"

Four-month-old Emily's mom was at her wits end trying to get Emily to fall asleep and stay that way. Her routine was to sit on a big bouncy ball with Emily on her lap and bounce her to dreamland. Then when Emily woke mid-way through her nap, her mom would repeat the process.

For the first few months, this process was tolerable and actually worked quite well. However, at around four-months-old, Emily began to waken more frequently during naps and the bouncing was not working anymore. Besides that, parents were exhausted in their attempts to help her fall asleep.

Emily's mom was ready to teach her to fall asleep on her own and stay asleep for her entire nap. She had read several books on the subject of sleep and tried every technique she had read about. Nothing seemed to be working and often times she didn't know exactly how to interpret the plans she was reading about. What she really needed was a consultant who could walk with her step by step and give her the customized type of help that she needed.

We began the process by helping Emily find something that was soothing to her. Quickly we noticed that she was beginning to find comfort in sucking her thumb. We encouraged Emily to self-soothe in this way, hoping she would use this skill to help her fall asleep initially for naps and nights as well as help her to fall back asleep mid-nap and during normal wakings during the night.

The first day on the plan was not easy for mom or for Emily. Emily had trouble falling asleep for naps and when she finally did, she would wake after 45 minutes. Emily was still tired after waking and would be fussy through the next cycle of feeding and play.

On the second day, however, Emily found great comfort in her thumb as we had hoped. She was able to soothe herself to sleep at the beginning of each nap, as well as fall back asleep after waking mid-nap. Nights also were a success.

SIDE NOTE: After several days on the plan, Emily's mom noticed that she was flipping herself over onto her stomach and unable to get herself back to her original position. To help correct this situation, she worked on the skill of flipping over during the day. She would gently assist her with the beginning of the flip by lifting up her leg and beginning the motion for her. Within a few days, Emily had the skill mastered and her mom was confident that Emily could easily and freely move in and out of any position while sleeping.

Happy Ending: Self-Soothing, not Mom-Soothing

This scenario might seem too good to be true, but one would be surprised to find that many babies respond this quickly and easily once they learn to soothe themselves to sleep. They find a thumb or stuffed animal very soothing and realize they are much better rested overall when they rely on themselves to fall asleep.

6

"Sweet Dreams"

Three to Seven Months

I remember right when my daughter turned 12 weeks old, I noticed she didn't seem as hungry at mealtimes. She had previously eaten very vigorously every 3 hours but suddenly only wanted to eat half of what she usually did. She also started to have trouble going down for naps when she had been so regular the previous week. What I began to realize was that as she grew older and bigger, she didn't need to eat as often and could be awake for longer periods of time. She was ready for an extended cycle of eating every four hours. I was really get excited about this phase because I knew it would last a long time compared to the previous couple of months.

Three to Five Months: Stretching out to a 4-hour cycle

During this time you are moving from a 2.5 or 3-hour routine to about every 4 hours during the day, and your baby is sleeping consistently 10 to 12 hours straight at night and taking three naps of 1.5 to 2 hours each. Again, it's normal for your baby to wake several times at night naturally, but she should be able to fall back to sleep on her own.

You will possibly be introducing solid foods at this point. Your pediatrician will offer you specific guidance. Remember to allot more time for meals as needed.

Sample schedule for Three to Five Months:

7 a.m.	Wake, eat, and play
9 a.m.	**Nap**
11 a.m.	Wake, eat, and play
1 p.m.	**Nap**
3 p.m.	Wake, eat, and play
5 p.m.	**Nap** (1.5 to 2 hours)
6:30 p.m.	Wake, eat, bedtime routine
8:30 p.m.	**Off to dreamland...**

Six to Seven Months:
Phasing out the 5 p.m. Nap

You might have been wondering for some time now why your child was fighting that last nap of the day. Well, you can breathe easy knowing that it is natural and expected.

During months five through seven, your baby will only need a catnap at the 5 p.m. nap instead of the 1.5- to 2-hour nap they were used to when they were younger. Limit the catnap to 45 minutes max or it can interfere with nighttime sleep. Once they don't seem tired for that nap or it is just for a few minutes, you can eliminate that nap and just put them down earlier for the night. This transition will be very gradual, natural, and easy to adjust to.

Sample Schedule for Six to Seven Months (with a detailed Bedtime Routine):

7 a.m.	wake, eat, and play
9 a.m.	**Nap**
10:30 or 11	wake, eat, and play
1 p.m.	**Nap**
2:30 or 3	wake, eat, and play
5 p.m.	**Nap** (30 to 60 min, gradually shorter over time)
6:00 p.m.	Bath/Change into Pajamas
6:45 p.m.	Last Milk Feeding
7:15 p.m.	Read three short stories (nursery rhymes are soothing for this age)
7:40 p.m.	Bedtime Prayers and Final Hugs
8:00 p.m.	Off to dreamland...

Tales from the Trenches:

"Double the Trouble but Double the Fun!"

Five-month-old twins, Carol and Elizabeth, were not getting enough rest during the day or night. They occasionally took naps but many days went all day without any rest. If they did take a nap, it was after much rocking, swaying, and bouncing to the point of sound sleep but only to wake after 20 to 30 minutes. A rare one-hour nap was celebrated once in a while. The girls were fussy most of the day.

Nights weren't much better. Although the girls did sleep up to 7 to 10 hours at night, their bedtimes were unpredictable, sometimes staying up until 11 p.m. They were also awakening multiple times a night for a bottle. Mom and dad were exhausted around the clock and desperate for some help. When they brought up the issue of sleep with their family pediatrician his response was "Maybe they just don't need that much sleep."

In the first stage of intervention, we worked on getting the girls on a three-hour feeding schedule. Most four-month-olds can handle 4 hours between feedings, but since the girls were accustomed to eating every 1.5 to 2 hours, we used a more gradual approach.

Over the course of the next couple weeks, Carol and Elizabeth's parents worked hard to get the girls on a three-hour schedule, doing what they could to get the girls more satisfied with each feeding in order to increase the time between feedings. Within a few days they were able to get them to eat every 3 hours and take up to 4 to 5 ounces at a time. In the next week or so, they were able to get the girls down for occasional one-hour naps a couple times a day. Elizabeth seemed to take to the schedule a little easier, but both were making great progress.

Just as the girls were getting more regular with feedings and sleep, the family's move to a new home interfered with the progress they had made. Also, with their parents' returning to work and them being with several different caregivers, Carol and Elizabeth lost the consistency of their routine and schedule.

After the family settled into their new home and were ready to become consistent again with their schedule, we began to bring some routine back into their lives. Now that they were a couple months older, starting on solids, and drinking more in one sitting, we moved to a four-hour schedule, which the girls took to nicely.

Elizabeth began drinking 6-8 ounces at each meal as well as eating the equivalent of one jar of baby food mixed with 4-5 tablespoons of cereal. Getting filled up at each meal during the day worked wonders for Elizabeth and she began sleeping 10-11 hours at night without waking. In the first few nights, she woke and cried for a short time, but when her parents allowed her to re-settle and soothe herself to sleep instead of immediately offering her a bottle and getting her system used to eating at night, it worked wonders.

Carol, on the other hand, still struggled with wanting to snack her way through the day and consequently wake at night for multiple feedings. Although her two lengthy daytime naps were consistently at the same time each day, her nights were still an issue for a while longer than expected. It took another couple months, but eventually her night time sleep was as solid as her sister's.

Happy Ending: No Carbon Copies!

In this case study, it is important to note that although both Carol and Elizabeth were on the same plan, the time that it took to find success varied according to personality and needs. Also, due to unforeseen changes (moving homes), the process took longer than expected. However, although progress was slower than desired or expected, both girls eventually came around once their lives were settled and the plan was back in place. Lastly, notice that persistence is really what pays off.

7

"Forty Winks"

Eight to Eighteen Months

Up until this point, the schedule changes pretty regularly over the months. Now you can finally take a big sigh of relief and enjoy the next 10 months or so when your baby will be on essentially the same schedule.

Finally: Stability!

Your child will probably only need two naps: one morning nap at around 10 a.m. and another at 3 p.m. and could very well sleep at night from 7 p.m. to 7 a.m. Yes, you read that correctly! That's 12 hours. There will be slight variance in babies, give or take an hour or two in a 24-hour period, but the pattern is the same.

At this age, your child's schedule will be gradually merging with family mealtime. It's a wonderful season of eating together as a family and is a new adventure! Offer the same foods for the entire family as much as possible and teach your child to appreciate a variety of foods. Resist the temptation to make many different meals for each member of the family. You are not a short order cook!

It's never too early to teach your child mealtime manners. As soon as they are eating, they should slowly be learning conventions and what is appropriate and polite at the table. It's a wonderful time to introduce sign language to help avoid frustration over mealtime issues such as being "hungry", wanting "more", or saying "thank you" or "please."

In the beginning of this stage, your child will be ready to eat a little bit early (around 4:30 to 5:30) and if that is too early for your family to dine together, consider offering light, healthy finger foods earlier in the evening and then offering the bulk of the meal (meats, milk, etc.) later when the entire family is together.

Sample Schedule for Eight to Eighteen Months

7 a.m.	Breakfast and play
10 a.m.	**Nap**
11:30 or 12	Lunch and play
3 p.m.	**Nap**
4:30 or 5	Dinner, and play
6:30 p.m.	Bedtime routine
7 or 8 p.m.	Off to dreamland...

Tales from the Trenches:

"Hungry at Night"

Little eight-month-old Aaron was waking once at night for a bottle at around 3 a.m. in the morning. His parents were convinced that he was waking because he was hungry and they felt obligated to continue to feed him each night. However, there eventually came a point where Aaron's parents questioned if things could be different. They wondered if there was a way to eliminate those night feedings.

First we worked on getting Aaron on a good daytime routine with enough rest and food. At eight-months-old, he was ready to eat three meals a day with his family and then take one bottle at night right before being tucked in. Our goal was to have Aaron's appetite satisfied during the day along with enough rest so that the need to wake at night would be eliminated.

During the first few days on the plan, Aaron continued to wake regularly at 3 a.m. for a feeding. Instead of immediately offering a bottle of milk, however, his parents waited 5 to 10 minutes to see if he would go back to sleep. If he was still awake after 10 minutes, then they gave him a bottle of water. The first night, Aaron drank just a few ounces and then went back to sleep. Each night he drank less and on the fourth night, Aaron no longer woke to feed during the night.

Happy Ending: Don't accept the status quo

The tricky part of this type of situation is that if babies grow accustomed to night feedings they can continue to waken out of habit more so than out of need. It may seem they are waking out of hunger and that they genuinely have a physical need. However, consider the possibility that they are, in fact, waking more out of habit and have trained their bodies to eat at a particular hour during the night, thereby creating a perceived need. Remember the example earlier in the book that demonstrates

Sleep Tight

how even adults can be trained to wake hungry in the middle of the night if a habit is developed.

Substituting water for milk causes the stomach to be less full and satisfied, therefore, causing babies to conclude it's not worth the hassle to get up. It also gives their systems an opportunity to get hungry enough for the first feeding in the morning, which begins a healthy cycle of having three satisfying meals during the day.

8

"Snug as a Bug in a Rug"

Two to Five Years

Your child is mobile now and needs lots of physical activity as well as a variety of other activities incorporated into his day. Try weekly library story hour, Mommy and Me classes at your local junior college, tumbling classes, time at the park or walks around the neighborhood, and socializing with others his age. Getting adequate stimulation and activity during the day will set the stage for sound and welcome rest at night.

18 to 30 Months:
Moving to One Nap

It's possible that at the beginning of this stage, your child will still need two naps during the day and 10 to 12 hours sleep at night. In that case, aim for a morning and afternoon nap lasting 1.5 to 2 hours each. Do your best to end the afternoon nap by 4 p.m. at the latest as to not interfere with nighttime sleep. Remember that

7:00 to 8:30 p.m. remains the optimal window for bedtime. If you find your child not tired at this time, think about waking him earlier in the morning.

Sometime during this period, your child will only need one long 2 to 3 hour nap after lunch. Again, do your best to end the nap by 4 p.m. at the latest so as to not interfere with nighttime sleep. Studies show that it is optimal for children to begin their nighttime sleep in the 7:00 to 8:30 p.m. window. Generally speaking, children who go to bed later tend to be more over-stimulated, don't sleep as soundly at night, wake earlier in the morning, and don't function as well during the day.

Suzy's Tip #7:

From Two Naps to One

As your child is transitioning from two naps to one, it's possible that for a few months what might work best is a short 45 minute nap in the morning around 9:30 or 10 a.m. and then a longer 2 hour nap in the afternoon around 2 to 4 p.m. until your child can happily get through the morning without rest. Another option is to alternate taking one nap and two naps for a while. For instance, your child might take one nap on M, W, and F and then take two on Tu, Th and/or on the weekends. Take tiredness and alertness signals from your child to decide what is needed.

For some children, it may work to shift this bedtime an hour or two earlier or later to adapt to the family's needs. However, it is important to mention that this schedule is not the ideal. See Chapter 9 for a Q and A on this topic.

Tales from the Trenches:

"Too Old and Set in His Ways?"

Eighteen-month old James was had a lot of good things going for him. He was predictably tired at the same time each day for nap and each evening for bedtime. Once his mom nursed and rocked him to sleep, he drifted off to sleep with no problems at all. He had been this way for many months and James' mom was very happy with the routine they had established.

After being so predictable and easy to manage, suddenly and with no forewarning, one day James decided that he would wake multiple times at night and mid-nap, requiring his mom to nurse him back to sleep repeatedly. Even with multiple interventions, James no longer was able to stay asleep after being put to sleep. After checking for teething or signs of illness or growth spurts, James' mom decided that what James needed was to learn the skill of self-soothing so that he could put himself to sleep and get back to sleep after all his natural mid-nap and nighttime wakings.

Since James was old enough to understand quite a bit of language, we began by talking to James and preparing him for what was ahead. We began by reassuring him of his mom's love and how proud she was of how much he was growing and maturing. We told him about how "big boys" learn to sleep on their own and stay asleep, just like daddy who is so big and strong. Then, we told him step by step the plan we had for the days ahead. Beginning with explaining he would not be nursed before naps and night and how he would learn to soothe himself to sleep and then fall back asleep after waking. We gave him a special "big boy sleep bear," set a fan in his room for background noise, and set to work.

Nervously, James' mom put him down for his nap on the first day after a few soothing stories in his bedroom rocking chair. She kissed him and lay him down calmly and quickly and then zipped out the door. Before she could even leave the room, she heard him rustling to stand up and begin to cry and call out for her despite the fact that he had been in a perfectly drowsy state before being put down.

She ran to the video monitor to watch James, and seeing that he was safe and still drowsy (rubbing his eyes and yawning between cries), she put her mind to the short task of folding some clothes. Only five minutes into her task, she heard James' crying shift from a full cry to more of a complaining cry. She glanced at the monitor and saw that he was lying down and breathed a sigh of relief as she went back to her folding. By the time she was done (5 minutes later), her son was silent and completely asleep to her amazement. For the next hour he was sound asleep and she was thinking this was all too easy, wondering why she hadn't tried this sooner.

Exactly one hour after James had fallen asleep his mom began to hear crying again. She checked the monitor and James was standing again and this time, calling "Mama! Mama!" over and over again. Although the words tugged at her heart, knowing he was safe and knowing that his naps were usually at least two hours long she decided to wait it out a bit to see if he would put himself back to sleep.

After 10 minutes of hard crying, she felt so confused and was tempted to throw in the towel and try again another day. She doubted the process and whether it was going to work for her son. In desperation she called me to ask for advice. After listening to his cries over the monitor (off and on crying) and seeing that he still looked tired, we decided to wait a few more minutes before making a decision about ending the nap. She began to explain to me step by step the process of how James went down for nap, the success of falling asleep on his own for the first time and staying asleep for an hour, but also the reservations she had about the whole experience. Within the first 5 minutes of her telling me the story, we heard James settle down little by little and by the time she finished her story, he was lying down and sound asleep again. He slept for a total of 3 hours that nap and all on his own!

Each day after this first experience, James went down progressively easier each night. Although he did continue to wake and even cry for a minute or two the next couple days, by the fourth day he was going down quietly and sleeping soundly for three hours straight on his own. At age 3.5, he still took three-hour daytime naps and slept 10-11 hours at night.

Happy Ending: Old Kids CAN Learn New Tricks

Remember that this is just one example of what could happen with an eighteen—month-old. Children are all individuals and the process will look differently for many children. In the end children can sleep anywhere from 1 hour to 3 hours for naps. What we are looking for is a child who is refreshed and able to be alert and content for 3-4 hours after waking for a smooth transition into the bedtime routine. Sometimes the process takes longer or there is a pattern of one step forward and two steps backward, which is also still within the realm of normal. As long as there is steady progress towards your ultimate goal, that is considered success!

Sleep Training an Older Child

Unfortunately, many parents are advised that if their child is into his third or fourth year of life, that he cannot learn new sleep habits. These poor parents resign themselves to sleepless nights while silently vowing to themselves that "next time, we will start earlier!"

If your child is two years old or older, and has not yet learned the art of sleeping, don't be discouraged. It is not too late. Yes, it will be more work, and you may find more resistance or challenges, but with your commitment and hard work, success too can be yours.

Since each situation is unique and your child has had some time to develop sleep habits over a longer period of time, below are sample scenarios that you might find speak to your situation. It could be that taking tips from a combination of scenarios might create the perfect solution for your child. Be open, flexible, and always use your parental gut. It is there for a reason.

However, once you commit to a solution, give it a good several weeks to consistently apply. Some children might need gradual change towards a goal and others might benefit from going it cold turkey. Wisely choose what you think will be best for everyone involved.

The Preschool Years: An Occasional Siesta

Somewhere around the age of four or five, children begin to not need to nap during the day. It may begin with a child only needing a shorter nap of about 45 minutes to one hour. Perhaps, for some time afterwards, she might need a nap every other day or even just a few times a week. For a period of time while she is still napping, it could mean a later bedtime. Then, after dropping the nap or on the days she doesn't nap, she would go down earlier at night. For instance, one day three-year-old Ashley takes a nap from 2:00-3:00 p.m. and then is not tired for bedtime until 9:30 p.m. that night. The following day she does not nap at all and is ready for bedtime by 7:30 p.m. With this in mind, Ashley's parents have the luxury of some flexibility. If they know the family will be out later one evening, they can plan on giving Ashley a nap, while on days they plan to be home and need some extended adult time, they can plan on keeping Ashley up during the day.

There you have it. A routine for each stage of childhood. If you haven't yet had a chance to look at Part Three, then please do so now. You'll find a grab bag of frequently asked questions. It's the next best thing to sitting around the table with a group of other parents.

PART THREE:

Smoothing Out the Wrinkles

Handling Challenges

O Bed! O Bed! Delicious Bed!
That heaven upon earth to the weary head.

−*Thomas Hood*

9

"Sleep on It"

General Q and A

Start Training During Day Or Night?

Q: "Is it best to start with training at night or during the day?"

A: Optimally, it is best to train around the clock. That means it's a good idea to teach your child each time they are put down to sleep whether it is for a nap or for the night. However, some parents find it easier to concentrate their efforts on nighttime first since that can be more crucial, especially if it is affecting the entire family's ability to sleep. Be encouraged that often times, once a child is trained at night, the skills will naturally transfer over to daytime naps. In the case that it doesn't, most likely a quick 3- to 5-day training period during the day is all that will be required.

No Success Within 3-5 Days

Q: "What if I don't have success within that 3 to 5 day period that you are talking about?"

A: The first night will quite possibly feel like the longest night in your parenting history. The second night should be at least slightly better and most times, the third night is a turn-around night, especially if your baby is six months or younger. It does get harder and take a bit longer for older children sometimes, but don't be discouraged. Take it one step at a time. It's possible that progress will not come as quickly or predictably as you'd like, but try to think long-term and evaluate soundly with a trusted friend or spouse with whom you share principles and conviction.

Use Of Baby Monitors

Q: "Do you recommend using baby monitors?"

A: An investment in a video monitor is highly recommended. Not only will it bring reassurance as you not only hear but also see that your child is safe and sound, it will be a tool that can be used for years to come as baby goes from crib to bed and sharing a room with a sibling, for instance. One word of advice, however, keep the volume down as it tends to exaggerate the sound. Unless a floor or many hallways separate you, if your child needs you, you will either see or hear it without the aid of the volume on a monitor.

Not Working After 7 Days

Q: "What if it's been a solid 7 days and it just doesn't seem to be working?"

A: Re-read the How-To Process and evaluate areas that may need adjustment. Chances are that in your tired daze, inconsistency or lack of follow-through is the culprit. Talk through your situation with your spouse or a trusted friend.

If you need a break, take one. Try the whole process over again in a week or so. For some, it just clicks the second time around. Don't be discouraged. Make tomorrow Day #1.

Lastly, consider getting a doctor's evaluation on whether your child has some physical condition such as sleep apnea, that is hindering their ability to get a good night's rest. Doctors say that snoring and erratic sleeping (lots of tossing, turning, and sudden jerks awake) can be signs of problems. Only after a condition is evaluated and treated will your child get the rest she needs.

Sleep Props

Q: "Are there sleep props that are okay for my child to keep?"

A: I would do away with bottles, breastfeeding, pacifiers, and rocking. As far as special blankets, teddy bears, or other routines, you will have to decide on that yourself. You just have to be okay with buying a dozen of the exact same blanket just in case and leaving one at grandmas, the sitter's, the car, the plane, the...You get my point.

Soothing Child During Training Process

Q: "Will it help if I go in to soothe my child and reassure him during the process?"

A: It's possible that intervening in the process to soothe or reassure your child can help. For some a quick and quiet visit with a soothing word and pat can do wonders. For many, however, any intervention is a false hope that can aggravate the situation further and bring you back to square one. Be sensitive to your individual situation and stick with what seems to be working. However, be sure you are giving it a good solid week before evaluating whether something is working or not.

Will We Always Be Slaves To A Schedule?

Q: "It is hard to imagine always having to schedule parties, swim classes, and all events around my baby's schedule. Will we ever be free from this?"

A: It is true that while you are establishing your baby's routine and sleep schedule, you should be very consistent and not stray from the routine as much as possible. Hopefully, you will see the predictability of the routine as more of a comfort than something that is enslaving you. Also, once your child's routine is established, you can stray from the routine for a short period of time for a class or a party as long as you come back to the routine. Depending on your child's flexibility and personality, you'll have to judge what you can get away with. Of course, as your child goes through teething and/or sickness, you will need to adjust things for a brief period of time. Again, come back to the routine and your child should welcome it back easily.

Working With Other Caregivers

Q: "My daughter is in daycare during the day and with me only in the evenings. If my caregiver is unwilling to help with daytime nap schedule and/or training, will my work at nighttime be sabotaged?"

A: It is optimal for your child to have consistency throughout the day as well as during the evening, but for many parents, this is not possible. When discussing your situation with your daytime caregiver, consider offering the reasons why you want to make this change. Wouldn't it be wonderful if she would be won over and apply the techniques to all the children in her care? Don't dismiss this possibility by not approaching the subject deliberately. In sharing your success at night and with your caregiver seeing the difference it has made in your child, she might be more open than you think.

If all attempts fail and there are no better options for your child's care with someone who can be on the same page with you, then there is still encouraging news for you. Many babies can learn the difference between what is acceptable at home and acceptable elsewhere. It is entirely possible that your child will sleep one way during the day and another way during the night and be all right with that. Or, it may be that you will need to do some re-training each weekend. The hope is that your efforts at home will produce such great powerful fruit, that the effects will begin to spill over into the daytime as well- with or without a caregiver's help.

Staying Up Late To Wait For Parent

Q: "Is it ever okay for me to allow my child to stay up later than that 7:30-8:30 p.m. window you were talking about? My husband comes home late from work and if my child went to sleep at 7:30 p.m., she'd never see her dad!"

A: Quality time with Dad is a high priority, so I'm glad you're concerned about this issue. In situations like yours, many parents have found that it works well to move the entire schedule an hour or so later. However, when there are older school-aged children in the house, their morning schedule will make it difficult to sleep in. In that case, you might need to be more creative. Make breakfast time Daddy time, or make good use of email, photos, and web chat.

Suddenly Waking For No Known Reason

Q: "What if for no known reason, my child wakes after having successfully learned to sleep on his own?"

A: If you have ruled out all other obvious options (teething, sickness, adjusting to new nanny, etc.), then consider that your child is just going through a normal learning process or testing a little bit to see how serious you are about this whole thing. I know you want to hear another solution here, but basically you need to go back to training as you did in the beginning. Don't be discouraged, however, because it will almost certainly be easier and quicker than the first time around. In no time, you will all be sleeping tight once again.

Older Child Being Woken By Crying Baby

Q: "I'm worried about my older child being woken up by the baby while I am training. What can be done about this?"

A: If your child has siblings that you are worried will be awakened during this training period, I have two words of advice. First of all, talk to your child about what you are doing and assure them it is okay to fall back asleep even if they hear their younger sibling crying. Even if your older child's sleep is disturbed, remember that we are only talking about a few days; a week at the most, so encourage him to hang in there for a few more days. Secondly, consider using white noise in the form of a talk radio station or sound machine (ocean or rain sounds) to block out the disruptions. You can even put one in each child's room.

10

"Out Like a Light"

Q and A for Birth to 18 Months

Still Seems Hungry At Night

Q: "I know my baby is old enough to sleep through the night and not need night feedings, but at eight months, he still wakes two times for a bottle. We can't seem to break this habit. Letting him cry doesn't seem to work. Is there a more gradual approach that we could try?"

A: Sometimes when an older baby has grown accustomed to night feedings, it is very difficult to break the habit without a lot of crying over many nights. For whatever reason, if you are unable to endure the tears, here are some ideas for a more gradual approach:

1. First, make sure your baby is getting enough to eat during the day. At eight months, he should be having 3 meals a day

with milk and solids. Some babies also enjoy one more liquid feeding before bedtime. Especially if you are struggling with night feedings, it's a good idea to give this last feeding.

2. Next, each time your baby wakes in the middle of the night, try to wait about 10 minutes to see if he will settle and fall back asleep. If he doesn't, attempt other ways to help soothe your baby to sleep before you offer the bottle. Without picking him up, try soft music, or a pat on the back or stroke on the head. Some babies even like a little wiggling of the crib.

3. As a last resort, offer water or watered down milk because it's less filling and satisfying and therefore less apt to interfere with daytime hunger.

4. Work to reduce the number of times you offer the bottle as well as the amount you offer over the course of a week.

Adding Rice Cereal To Bottle

Q: "What do you think about adding some rice cereal into my month old baby's bottle? My friend say it will fill up his tummy and keep him asleep longer during the night."

A: Be careful to introduce any solids to a newborn baby. Doctors do not recommended to introduce cereals until at least the fourth month of life. Once your baby is of age, foods should be introduced one at a time for three to five days in a row to check for allergic reactions. Also, contrary to popular belief, adding cereal to your baby's' bottle will not make your baby sleep longer at night.

Use Of Pacifier

Q: "My child used to fall asleep within a few moments after putting the pacifier in her mouth. It was a source of comfort to both my daughter and myself because it was such a reliable prop to get her to sleep. However, this changed one night. After a few months, she started waking in the middle of the night and wanting her pacifier because it had fallen out of her mouth. I found myself getting up over a dozen times during one night to put the pacifier back into her mouth but I cannot keep this up forever. Help!"

A: As you are discovering and as is true with many sleep props there comes a time when it is best to wean your child. **The way that your child falls asleep is what they are looking for when they start to stir or enter into lighter stages of sleep.** In the case of pacifier use during the night, it will take some time but your child can indeed learn to sleep without it. There are two ways to manage this. The quickest way is to just take the pacifier away cold turkey one night and be determined to not give it to your child when she wakes. Most likely within a few days, she will learn to fall asleep without it. If excessive crying for a few days is too much and you'd prefer to make it a longer and more gradual process, try this:

Let your child get to a calm state and begin to drift off (still body, eyes drooping or slightly opening and closing) with the pacifier in her mouth but before she gets into a deep sleep (rapid eye movement, heavy breathing, etc.) remove the pacifier immediately and put her down to sleep.

When she wakes at night, wait for 10 minutes or until the cries seem to be escalating. Then, give her the pacifier but remove it, again, once she starts drifting off.

Over the course of the next several days to weeks, gradually offer the pacifier less quickly and for shorter amounts of time. Your child will eventually realize it's just not worth the effort anymore.

Teething, Growth Spurt, Or Illness

Q: "What should I do if my child was sleeping well and then suddenly begins to wake due to teething, growth spurts, or illness?"

A: Chances are very high that if your child has learned the art of sleeping that discomfort from teething, growth spurts, or mild colds will interfere minimally with their sleep at night. However, if you find them suddenly waking from one of these discomforts, then do your best to soothe pain before bedtime with a pain reliever in consultation with your doctor. If your child does wake, then treat him as needed, but be careful not to bring in sleep props again. Rest assured, the challenges should only last 3 to 5 days or until the colds subside. For colds, try elevating the mattress with blankets underneath or use a humidifier or Vicks vapor rub. If you need to go into the room at night, make it as brief as possible. If wakings continue even after the situation is resolved, you will be dealing with wakings out of habit, not need. In this case, you know what to do, right?

If symptoms last longer than a week or your child seems to be in great discomfort especially when first being laid down, consult your doctor for evaluation. Your child could be battling an ear infection or other more serious physical condition.

Suzy's Tip #8:

"To Pacify or Not, That is a Question"

Many parents struggle with this question at one point or another. Here are some thoughts to help make the best decision for your baby and family.

1. Pacifier use in the first six weeks of life can interfere with successful breast-feeding so avoid use if you find suckling need is satisfied by the pacifier rather than at the breast.

2. Habits developed within the first few months of life are fairly easy to break as long as you are gradually weaning from dependence over time. The best way to handle this is to offer the pacifier only as a last resort and avoid using it to soothe baby at every moment of discomfort. Over time, there should be a pattern of less usage with the goal to be totally free from usage by the fourth month of life. That doesn't mean you can't break the habit after that time, but the longer you wait, the harder it will be.

3. Some babies are just as happy to suck on a finger after having used a pacifier for some time. Although some may disagree with this viewpoint, thumb sucking is a self-soothing tool and is preferable to the pacifier in the long run.

4. If a baby is used to having someone put a pacifier in his mouth in order to fall asleep, it is very likely that he will need that same help each time he wakes. It is normal for babies to wake multiple times during naps and nighttime. Teaching them to self-soothe back to sleep is crucial.

Waking At Night

Q: "My eight-month-old is still getting up in the middle of the night for a feeding. How do I know if he really needs to eat or if it's just a habit?"

A: In many cases, once babies reach 13 to 14 pounds they can go 8 to 10 hours or more without eating at night. Unless your eight-month-old is very petite or has other health issues that require frequent feedings around the clock, there is no reason you need to continue to feed him at night. Be sure to give him 3 solid feedings with solids each day as well as a liquid feeding right before bed and he should be able to make it until morning. Of course, it might take several days to teach his body not to wake in the middle of the night for feedings as he's been used to, but if you are consistent and persistent you all should be enjoying uninterrupted nights very soon.

In Own Bed For The First Time

Q: "We were happy with co-sleeping and breast feeding our daughter to sleep for the beginning period of parenting, but we are ready to move her into her own bed for the night without any sleep props. Can you help with this process?"

A: If your child has been used to co-sleeping for some time, you will probably need to be prepared for the possibility of a longer period of transition to sleeping alone. Work a step-by-step plan where you give each new habit in the process about 3 to 5 days on it's own to become routine. For instance, you might want to begin with weaning from breast-feeding right before bed. If you don't want to drop the bonding time completely, consider moving the time one hour earlier so that there is less of an association of breast feeding and falling asleep. Once this change is accomplished, move onto teaching your child to sleep in his own bed little by little.

How To Keep Routine During Travel

Q: "We are planning a big vacation in a few weeks and we are not sure how to make a smooth transition to sleeping in a different place. Any suggestions?"

A: Some babies transition very easily and others are more resistant. Allow for some flexibility in your schedule while you are away for it is very hard to keep everything completely consistent. However, here are some tips on helping to make it the most positive experience possible:

1. Take along familiar blankets, toys, and especially white noise to place right near the playpen. Even if you are sharing a room, this will help block out noises that will startle or wake your child.

2. If you are taking along a pack-n-play, have your child routinely sleep in it while you are at home for a few days before you leave on your trip. You can begin with naps and then eventually have him sleep in it every time he goes down, whether day or night.

3. Especially if you are sharing a room together, create a tall barricade around your child's sleeping area so that she will not be distracted by the activity or movement in the room. You can use a combination of furniture, blankets, and pillows to create this environment.

Baby Doesn't Settle Down For Bedtime

Q: "My baby seems ready to play and is still so active around the bedtime that you suggest. We can't seem to get him to that drowsy state you talk about. Do you have any recommendations?"

A: Some babies are easily stimulated and ready to play when they have had juice, sweet snack, or a stimulating activity right before bed. Do your best to create a soothing bedtime routine.

Create a quiet, dim, and soothing environment before bed. Turn off the TV and make it a habit for the last hour of the day to be quiet and calm. Your baby will take cues from this and be more likely to get into that drowsy state that is optimal.

If all else fails, consider shortening his last daytime nap by 30 minutes by either waking him early if he is sleeping 2 hours, or beginning it 30 minutes earlier.

Stands Up In Crib And Can't Sit Back Down; Rolls Onto Stomach And Can't Roll Back

Q: "My son just learned how to pull himself up to standing and is practicing this skill in his crib. The problem is he can't get himself back down so that he can fall asleep. What can I do to help him without going in his room over and over again?"

A: Learning to stand is a new and exciting skill that your child will want to practice over and over again. In order to give him the practice he needs and loves, consider providing many opportunities during playtime when he can enjoy this newfound skill. Also, work on teaching him to get back down after standing. Gently nudge the back of his legs to show him how to bend and plop down to the ground. The hope is that he will have enough practice during play time to satisfy his desire to practice this skill and also that if he does find the need to try out his skills in the crib, he will at least know how to get back down.

Also, if your child has an issue with rolling from one side (stomach to back or back to stomach) to another but not knowing how to roll back the other way, you can use the same approach as outlined above. Simply practice during playtime and in time he will learn.

Still Waking At Night After Teething Discomfort Has Subsided Or Cold Has Passed

Q: "My 18-month-old daughter was sleeping through the night prior to her teeth erupting but she began waking in the middle of the night due to teething pain. Now that her teeth are in, I don't know why she is still waking at night. Please help!"

A: We are creatures of habit. If you wake at 3 a.m. for a few nights in a row and receive soothing and maybe even a nice warm bottle because that is the only thing that soothes that 'ol achy tooth, then the mid night waking can be a hard habit to break even when that tooth isn't so achy anymore. Rest assured, however, that going back to the old routine of sleeping soundly all night can be rediscovered again within a few days. Assure your child before bedtime (they understand MUCH more than we give them credit for!) by explaining to them how you will see them in the morning. Tell them daddy, mommy, brother, and sister are all in bed too and that we will see everyone in the morning when the sun comes up. Explain to them it's okay to wake up but then to hug their bear really tight and go back to sleep. Tell them you won't be coming into the room anymore until morning but that you still love them and will look forward to seeing their bright face again in the morning. Then, do your best to allow children to soothe themselves back to sleep with no intervention if and when they wake in the middle of the night. The first night will be the hardest but by the third night most have easily gone back to their good old ways and welcome an uninterrupted full night's rest.

Suzy's Tip #9:

Natural Night Wakings:

Did you know that even adults wake several times at night and that this is normal? They stir, roll over, and then fall back asleep multiple times at night. What's not healthy, however, is staying awake each time one is awoken and needing outside help to fall back asleep.

Many times, parents are successful in getting their child to initially fall asleep on his own, but then when a child awakens, he cannot fall back to sleep without help. A child needs to learn to pass through the lighter cycles of sleep into the deeper stages without interruption. If he is used to relying on sleep props (rocking, feeding, singing, etc.) to fall asleep, then that's what he will look for each time he awakens.

11

"Early to Bed, Early to Rise"

Q and A for Eighteen Months to 4 years

Bed Wetting

Q: "My three-year-old just recently was potty-trained during the day but still wets his bed at night. It is such an ordeal changing and washing sheets and clothes in the middle of the night each night and we are at our wits end. Can you help?"

A: It is not unusual for nighttime training to come later than daytime. Especially for those children who are very deep sleepers, it is difficult to be roused enough to get to the restroom on time. Here are a couple suggestions to help with this process of training:

Limit liquids after dinnertime. Keep your children well hydrated during the day but encourage them to finish all their drinking at their last meal of the day. That means no huge cups of water after brushing their teeth or after being tucked into bed!

Waken your child to use the bathroom around 10-11pm before you head off to bed. Eventually you might find it becomes and routine and they will naturally wake to take care of their needs on their own.

Waking Too Early In Morning

Q: "My child wakes at 5:00 a.m. every morning because she needs to use the restroom. I can tell she is still tired and would have slept at least another hour or so if she had not needed to use the restroom. What can I do to help her sleep in longer in the morning?"

A: This is a very common problem you describe. It is often difficult for children to fall back asleep after waking with the sun. As children mature, however, often times they learn to sleep past these initial stirring early in the morning and wake at a more agreeable hour. In the meantime, here are a couple suggestions to help the process along:

1. Limit liquids after dinnertime. Keep your children well hydrated during the day but encourage them to finish all their drinking at their last meal of the day. That means no huge cups of water after brushing their teeth or after being tucked into bed!

2. Wake your child to use the restroom around 10 to 11 p.m. before you head off to bed. She'll be sleepy, so chances are the next morning she won't even remember having gotten up. Eventually you might find it becomes and routine and she will naturally wake to take care of her needs on her own.

From Crib To Bed

Q: "What's the best way to move my child from crib to bed?"

A: Keep your child in his crib for as long as is comfortable for him. When you feel comfortable that he can honor the boundary of staying in bed for a naptime (usually not until after age 2), then begin with these tips. Once you have success during the day, move to nighttime sleep, as well.

Use a twin size mattress on the ground to start. Toddler beds are options too, but if your child is eventually going to sleep in a twin bed, then it's a good idea to just begin the transition with one.

Move the crib blankets, stuffed animals, or other comforting items to the bed and put up a bed rail and some pillows to create a cozy and comfortable space for your child. For some children, a big twin bed is a shocking change and making the space smaller and more familiar can ease the transition.

Oftentimes, an impending sibling's arrival necessitates the move. In this case, be sure to have your child adjusted to the change months before the arrival of the baby. This way your child will be less likely to associate the change with adding a sibling to the family.

Adjusting To Daylight Savings Time

Q: "It takes us weeks to get adjusted to daylight savings time and I'd love to find a way to make the adjustment more gradual. Do you have any tips?"

A: Begin the adjustment early. A week before the official time change, gradually move your child's bedtime earlier or later by 15 minutes every couple nights. By the time you officially change your clocks, your child will already be used to the new bedtime and will be more likely to be right on the schedule you are all used to.

Four-Year-Old Can Get Out Of Bed and Walk To Parents' Room

Q: "What should I do when I am trying to train an older child to stay in his room all night when he can just get up and get out of bed whenever he wants?"

A: If you haven't already, you need to sit down and have a serious talk with your child about the expectations you have at nighttime as well as some specific consequences for not complying. Discuss how he needs to stay in his room all night and that you will see him when the sun comes up. For a safe and secure alternative to closing and locking his bedroom door, consider using a safety gate so that he can see out but cannot get out. Even if he falls asleep on the floor next to the gate the first couple nights, consider that a success. The goal is to stay in his room all night long and if he has succeeded, you can then work on getting him from the floor to his bed The hardest battle is over once he actually stays in his room all night. Of course, then you must brag about his accomplishments the next morning to everyone you come across. And, of course, he must always be within earshot when you do this.

Shift From Being An Only Child To An Older Sibling

Q: "My daughter is blaming her little brother for everything. She feels he has taken over her crib, highchair, stroller, and feels he is generally a nuisance more than a friend. What can I do to help?"

A: It is really important to prepare an older sibling for a new baby in the house. Do what you can to help them to feel it is a joy and privilege rather than an inconvenience and nuisance. Avoid saying things like, "You can't sleep in your crib anymore because the baby needs it." Instead, say, "Aren't you lucky that you're such a big girl that you get to sleep in a big bed now?" Read books on becoming a "Big Sister" or "Big Brother" and focus on the privileges that come with age.

Difference Between Nightmares And Night Terrors

Q: "What is the difference between a nightmare and a night terror? Should they be handled differently?"

A: Basically a nightmare is brief and your child will be awake and need consoling. In comparison, in a night terror, your child is actually still asleep and it is not wise to try to wake them. Instead, just be sure they are physically safe and wait it out with them until they settle back down to calm sleep. For more detailed information regarding the differences between nightmares and night terrors, consult chapter 10 of *Enjoy the Ride*.

Four-Year-Old Is Not Tired

Q: "My four-year-old is fighting his nighttime routine and complains that he is not tired. If we are lucky enough to get him into bed, he lies in bed up to an hour and plays. What can we do?"

A: If a three or four-year-old is getting sufficient regular physical activity, then most likely he will need a nap or rest during the day. That is a good thing for him and for his parents. However, if you are experiencing trouble with nighttime sleep, then perhaps your child is ready to drop that nap and head to bed earlier in the evening. Or, it could be that her nap needs to be shortened to just an hour or hour and a half. Lastly, be reminded that naps that end after 4 p.m. often extend a child's schedule and cause them to not be sleepy at that optimal 7:30 to 8:30 p.m. window. Optimal time for an afternoon nap or rest at this age is from about 1 to 3 p.m.

Son Expects Treats Before Cooperating

Q: "Once in a while, we would offer my son a treat in the morning if he did his bedtime routine cooperatively and went to bed without complaining. Now, however, he is starting to expect treats and rewards every time he goes to bed without complaining. How can we get out of this cycle?"

A: It is really tempting to bribe, I mean, offer your child an incentive to do a good job and the intention is well understood. However, it can often backfire as well as send the wrong message. Getting into a better nighttime routine and learning to sleep soundly on his own, is something that he is doing for himself and not for you. Be careful what you are communicating when you offer a treat for doing something that is really his responsibility.

There's a difference between a bribe and a celebration. The former is like dangling a bone in front of a dog to get them to come to you and the latter is like watching your dog do a bunch of tricks and then running up to him and giving him a big hug because you are so proud of him. So, with this analogy, I say, "Go ahead and celebrate," but don't bribe.

If you find that your child is already in the habit of expecting bribes for compliant behavior, the adjustment to doing something without external reward may not be easy. In this process, explain to your child what you are doing, stay determined and consistent, and know that although you may see strong resistance, the knowledge that this is what is best for your child in the long run should keep you on track. As you look back, you will see your child developing a sense of internal motivation and that is worth any short-term trials in teaching this lesson to your child.

Sleeping With Mom's Shirt

Q: "I've heard about people putting a parent's shirt on a teddy bear and then putting it in their child's crib. Can you explain the reasoning behind this?"

A: For an older child who seems to be taking the training a bit harder than most and is used to a year or more of sleeping with mom and dad, a bear with the familiarity of a parent can be a good transitional tool used to help comfort a child and ease them into sleeping on their own.

Daughter Comes To Our Room Every Night

Q: "My daughter does very well falling asleep in her own bed, but she knows where we sleep! Almost every night at around 3 a.m., she finds her way into our bedroom. How can we get her to stay in her bed all night long?"

Sleep Tight

A: When you are in a deep sleep and your child is quietly creeping into bed with you, it can be very difficult to think up a plan on the spot. Begin the conversation early in the day and reinforce your plan before tucking in at night.

Begin by talking to your child when you tuck her into bed and remind her to stay in her bed until she sees the morning light. List the people you know who also do the same thing: mommy, daddy, brother, sister, auntie, doggie, Corduroy, Elmo, Belle, etc. You get the idea. Give her a special teddy bear (perhaps with mommy's shirt and comforting scent on it) to hold when she wakes at night and let her know that is your way of being with her. Encourage her to hug her bear tightly and think of sweet things if she wakes in the middle of the night so that she will drift back off to sleep.

If this does not work, then every time, and I mean every time she comes to your bed take her back to her bed, even if it means you are doing it a dozen times for the first night. When she comes to your room, don't talk to her or hug her or make it an enjoyable encounter in any way. Just matter-of-factly, walk her back to her room, kiss her on the cheek and say, "See you in the morning," and then head back to your own room. If she returns, do it again...and again...and again...you have to be more committed than she is. She will try to wear you out, but hold fast to the dream of the night she doesn't come to you, and be the Energizer Bunny for these few nights.

If after a few nights there is no progress, then tell your child that if she continues to come to your bed at night, she will have to go back into a crib or playpen because only "big girls" sleep in "big beds" and they stay there all night long. For a short period of time, consider offering a small incentive to stay in bed until morning. Use small stickers on a chart (see the resource section of *Enjoy the Ride*) and then celebrate with going out to buy new fun bed sheets together! Avoid giving big rewards or prizes for something that she 'should' be doing anything. Celebrating with new sheets keeps the focus on the accomplishment and reinforces the behavior you are working on. After the goal is accomplished, use positive verbal reinforcement to express how proud you are of her accomplishment and talk about how wonderful it is for everyone in the family to get such nice rest all night long. This verbal encouragement and sense of accomplishment in your child should eventually replace any physical incentives. In this instance, although this technique may initially appear as a "bribe", if used very briefly and with the intent to put the focus back on the accomplishment, it can prove to be very effective.

Hopefully it won't come to this, but as a last resort, if all else fails, tell your child that if she continues to come into the room that she will not be allowed to come into your bed. Then, as hard as it is, you have to be consistent and not let her in. It could be that for a couple nights she will curl up on the floor next to you, but most likely she will realize her warm, cozy bed is a much better choice. I know I probably don't have to tell you this, but don't make a cozy corner in your room with a mattress on the floor, warm stuffed animals, and fluffy pillows awaiting your daughter. If you build it, she will come.

Consider whether your child's desire to sleep with you at night is a cry for quality time together. If you suspect this could be the case, spend regular time together that really feeds your child's spirit and see what a difference that can make.

Emotionally Damaging?

Q: "It's so hard when my son complains of nightmares or tells us he is afraid to go to bed. We worry that we are doing the wrong thing sending him to bed by himself. Is he being damaged emotionally by being required to sleep on his own?"

A: Nothing tugs at a parent's heart more than when they hear of their child's fear or insecurities. It's also normal to wonder if the training process is harming your child. Do your best to evaluate if your child is truly having nightmares or is using it as an excuse to delay bedtime. It is also important to determine if the protests are due to other reasons. It is crucial for all parents to have a network of support where they can rely on sound advice, so check in with others who know your family and situation when in doubt. In the end, listen to your parental gut. It is very reliable.

If you have ruled out all you can and your son is still complaining, consider if he is legitimately not tired and could move his bedtime a bit later. If he seems tired at too late an hour (9 p.m. or later), then consider waking him earlier in the morning. Depending on his age (see Sleep Average chart in appendix), it might be time to make an adjustment. Keep in mind, however, that although there is a range that is normal for a child, there is really not that much variance.

My Child Is Insecure From My Absence

Q: "I have been in the hospital for a solid month due to complications with the birth of my second child. During my absence, my older daughter has felt abandoned and so worried that she barely sleeps and clings to me in fear. What can be done?"

A: You might have a special circumstance where you feel that it would be detrimental to your child to follow the guidelines above and need some adaptation. It could be that your child has extreme separation issues due to a developmental stage or is missing you from being separated due to work, trip, or an extended illness. Or, it could be that your child has been sleeping with you for three years and an abrupt change in routine would not be the best. In these instances, try the following method to gradually ease your child into falling asleep on their own. It will mostly likely take longer than the method described earlier, but it can still be successful.

1. As described above, establish a soothing and regular bedtime routine with a bedtime in the 7:30 to 8:30 p.m. range.

2. Without worry in your voice, but with gentle confidence, assure your child that they are very capable and that you will help ease them into sleeping on their own. Talk about how everyone in the family sleeps in their own bed and bring excitement to the idea that they get their own bed and/or room, etc.

3. For the first night or two, take one step towards your eventual goal, and each night, gradually take one more step until you are where you want to be. The exact way this plays out and the time frame will vary depending on your situation., but plan to limit the training period to a few weeks at most.

For instance, if your child has been used to sleeping with you in your bed, then perhaps a first step is for both of you to move to sleep in your child's bed. Then, after a night or two, sit on the side of her bed while she falls asleep. Then, the next night, sit in a chair a foot away from her bed. Each night, gradually move further and further away from the bed and stay for a shorter amount of time until one night you kiss her goodnight and just walk out the door!

Whatever your situation, take time to make a specific plan that gradually brings you to where you want to be. Remember, that ideally, the process should be from one to three weeks. Any longer and you'll be so exhausted, you'll just want to crawl into your mother's bed!

Wetting Bed And Throwing Up In Protest

Q: "My child is getting so upset that he is wetting his pants and even throwing up in protest. Please help!"

A: Remember that your child is breaking some strong habits that have been ingrained for years and it will not be easy. Especially if outbursts such as these have worked in the past, don't expect them to dissolve quickly. Although this can be very upsetting for parents and cause them to give up on the whole battle, think long-term and press on. Go in and clean up what you need to with limited interaction, reassure your child matter-of-factly, then leave and continue the training. Your child will overcome these physical challenges after the first few instances. Be sure that you overcome the challenge of handling them, as well.

Weaning From Thumb Sucking

Q: "My child has sucked her thumb since she was in the womb and completely relies on it for sleep. Her pediodontist says, however, that she needs to stop, but we don't know how to go about it."

A: For many reasons, it's a good idea to get rid of the thumb sucking habit by age 5. As with breaking all habits, the longer you wait, the harder it will be, so if possible, earlier is best. Some ideas to divert the habit include using bitter nail polish or special appliances for the mouth. Consult your dentist for the latter of these options.

It also helps if your child is on the same page as you. By age 5, they can begin to understand the detriment thumb sucking can do to their teeth and can partner with you in breaking this habit. Subtle reminders such as a painted thumbnail, band-aid, or even a glove (especially helpful at night) can be helpful. In some situations, it is helpful to assist your child in finding something that would satisfactorily substitute thumb sucking. For instance, if he sucks his thumb when needing consolation, suggest he come for a hug from mom and dad or cuddle up with a favorite stuffed animal. However, use wisdom in keeping everything in perspective and balance.

12

"Sleep Tight and Wake Bright"
Final Thoughts

If you come to this last chapter as someone who has gone through the journey of teaching your child to sleep through the night and have restful daytime rest, then congratulations! Things must definitely be looking brighter for you, as well as your child. You've pressed through doubts and worries, and stuck to the plan to make it to this point. You're breathing a huge sigh of relief and wondering why you had waited this long to try! Enjoy your success and then look around you and reach out to another parent who is in the same predicament you were just a short while ago. Share with them your struggles and successes and encourage them in their own journey of teaching their child the art of sleep.

As you relish in this newfound energy (amazing what a good night's rest can do for a parent, right?), and as you continue on this road, keep your mind focused on the long-term goal. Bumps along the road are inevitable. Your child will probably backtrack at some point along the way and you will doubt whether the same process will work again, but rest assured that it will. Most of the time, it will only take a fraction of the time it took originally and you will all be back on the road to rest before you know it. Always remember that sleep is an essential part of life and teaching your child to sleep is a gift that will last a lifetime. Any short-term discomfort will be worth it in the end.

As your child enters the school years, the foundations you've laid for healthy habits and good self-discipline will serve you and your child well. Even though your sleep training is complete, your work as a parent has many more chapters to come.

Let me take a moment to speak to those of you who come to this chapter still a skeptic. You've skimmed through the pages and even come back to parts of it, but you just don't feel ready or you're not sure if it's "right" for you and your child. That's okay. This plan is not for everyone, and until you are sure and committed to give it a try you should not plan to try it half-heartedly. That would be a disservice to you and your child. However, let me say that if you have made it this far in the book then chances are you almost at a point where you are ready to commit. If this is the case, take the next step. Ask the questions. Reach out for help. Talk to someone who has been through this process successfully and gain encouragement and support. You'll know when you're ready, and when you are, *Sleep Tight* will be here for you.

Now that I've exhausted everyone (including myself) on the topic of sleep, I think I will turn in now and say, "Sleep tight, wake bright, and don't let the bedbugs bite!" May you all sleep peacefully, knowing that your child is doing the same. See you in the morning!

I will both lay me down in peace, and sleep:
for thou, Lord, only makest me dwell in safety.

–Psalm 4:8

Resources

Infant Feeding / Sleep Log
Summary of Sleep Routines
Lullabies

You can always find more great resources and ideas at www.MothersFriendSOS.com

Infant Feeding / Sleep Log

Time feed-ing began	Time since last feed-ing	Duration (if breast-feeding)		Amount (if bottle feeding)	Wet Diapers	Dirty Diapers	Sleep Hr:min
		R	L	oz.			
		R	L	oz.			
		R	L	oz.			
		R	L	oz.			
		R	L	oz.			
		R	L	oz.			
		R	L	oz.			
		R	L	oz.			
		R	L	oz.			
	totals:			oz.			

Summary of Sleep Routines, Birth to Five Years

Age	Daytime Hours Slept	# of Naps	Nighttime Hours Slept	# of Meals	Total Hours Slept
0 to 4 weeks	8	4	8	7 to 8	16
After baby drops midnight and 3 a.m. feedings:					
5 to 8 weeks	6.5	4	9	5 to 6	15.5
Once child has stretched to a four-hour cycle:					
3 to 5 months	4.5	3	10.5	4	15
When third nap becomes a catnap:					
6 to 7 months	3.5	3	11	4	14.5
When child drops evening nap:					
8 to 18 months	3	2	11.5	3	14.5
When child drops morning nap:					
18 – 30 months	2.5	1	11.5	3	14
When child drops afternoon nap:					
By 5 years	0	0	11.5	3	11.5

Note: All ages and times above reflect our general goals. Individual children may reach each phase at a slightly different age and may require up to an hour more or less of sleep per day.

Lullabies

Beyond "Twinkle"

Even if you're not Aretha Franklin or Josh Groban, your baby loves to hear you sing. There are few things on this earth more comforting than the gentle melody of a mother or father's song. Don't let your child miss out on this wonderful part of childhood. You probably know the tunes to the songs below. Here are the words, just to get you started.[4]

Hush Little Baby

Hush, little baby, don't say a word.
Papa's gonna buy you a mockingbird
And if that mockingbird won't sing,
Papa's gonna buy you a diamond ring
And if that diamond ring turns brass,
Papa's gonna buy you a looking glass
And if that looking glass gets broke,
Papa's gonna buy you a billy goat
And if that billy goat won't pull,
Papa's gonna buy you a cart and bull
And if that cart and bull turn over,
Papa's gonna buy you a dog named Rover
And if that dog named Rover won't bark
Papa's gonna buy you a horse and cart
And if that horse and cart fall down,
You'll still be the sweetest little baby in town.

---

[4] All lyrics are public domain. The songs listed here and more are available at www.babycentre.co.uk.

Brahms' Lullaby

Lullaby and good night, with roses bedight
With lilies o'er spread is baby's wee bed
Lay thee down now and rest, may thy slumber be blessed
Lay thee down now and rest, may thy slumber be blessed

Lullaby and good night, thy mother's delight
Bright angels beside my darling abide
They will guard thee at rest, thou shalt wake on my breast
They will guard thee at rest, thou shalt wake on my breast

Day Is Done (Taps)

Day is done,
Gone the sun,
From the lake, from the hills, from the sky.
All is well, safely rest, God is nigh.

All Through the Night

Sleep my child and peace attend thee,
All through the night
Guardian angels God will send thee,
All through the night
Soft the drowsy hours are creeping,
Hill and dale in slumber sleeping,
I my loved ones' watch am keeping,
All through the night

Angels watching, e'er around thee,
All through the night
Midnight slumber close surround thee,

All through the night
Soft the drowsy hours are creeping,
Hill and dale in slumber sleeping
I my loved ones' watch am keeping,
All through the night

For those of you who are more confident in your vocal prowess, there are some wonderful classic songs that make great lullabies. Due to copyright restrictions, we can't share the lyrics here, but feel free to consult your favorite music store. Better yet, delve into your mp3 collection and get creative!

Goodnight, My Someone – from The Music Man
Summertime – from Porgy and Bess
Golden Slumbers – The Beatles
Blackbird – The Beatles
A Nightingale Sang in Berkeley Square – Nat "King" Cole *et al*
Moon River – Andy Williams and others
"Over the Rainbow" – from "The Wizard of Oz"
What a Wonderful World – Louis Armstrong
When You Wish Upon a Star – from Pinnochio

Do you have a favorite lullaby that we left off the list? We'd love to hear from you. Visit www.MothersFriendSOS.com and click on the link that says "Email Suzy."

Reference

Index of "Suzy's Tips"

Index of Charts

Index of Questions and Answers

Main Index

.

Parents, Teachers, and Caregivers:
Invite Suzy Martyn to speak at your next event.

With warm wit and inspiring stories, Suzy equips her audiences to successfully manage the toughest challenges including:

- **Motivating picky eaters** to make healthful choices
- **Getting to the root of anger** in a child and helping manage it
- **Instilling a sense of responsibility** and a good work ethic
- **Setting limits** in firm, yet loving ways
- **Teaching your child the art of sleep** so you can get some rest
- **Potty-training your two-year-old** with simplicity and low stress
- **Motivating your children to joyfully get along**
- **Conquering your unique parenting challenges**

Suzy provides personalized
one-on-one coaching

She will walk with you through your unique situation so that you can meet your parenting goals and start to "Enjoy the Ride" of parenting.

To invite Suzy to speak in your community, request personalized help, follow her blog, and read reviews, please visit:

Website: www.MothersFriendSOS.com

E-mail: suzy@mothersfriendsos.com

About the Author

For 25 years, Suzy Martyn has been caring for children in the classroom, in her home childcare, through her parenting consultation service, and with her three daughters. Serving as a keynote speaker for Babies "R" Us and Mothers of Preschoolers, she shares her knowledge and experience with parents all over southern California. Her advice has appeared in national parenting magazines, as well as in her monthly column "Parent Matters" for the Orange County Event News. Suzy holds a Masters in Education specializing in language acquisition, an Advanced Bachelor's degree in Liberal Studies, a Multiple Subject Teaching Credential, and a Language Development Certificate.

Suzy lives in Orange County, CA with her husband of 17 years and their three daughters, ages 13, 11, and 8.